You and Your Relationship Journey

How to Navigate Difficult Relationships, Step into Your Power, and Make Healthy Choices

WENDY J. BRITTEN

BALBOA.PRESS
A DIVISION OF HAY HOUSE

Balboa Press books may be ordered through booksellers or by contacting:

Balboa Press
A Division of Hay House
1663 Liberty Drive
Bloomington, IN 47403
www.balboapress.com.au
AU TFN: 1 800 844 925 (Toll Free inside Australia)
AU Local: (02) 8310 7086 (+61 2 8310 7086 from outside Australia)

Print information available on the last page.

ISBN: 978-1-9822-9598-1 (sc)
ISBN: 978-1-9822-9599-8 (e)

Balboa Press rev. date: 10/25/2022

CONTENTS

DEDICATION

To my mother, who through her life and suffering planted the seed of what is important in life.

ACKNOWLEDGEMENTS

I have several people to thank who supported me through the process of getting this book out into the world, some who I have never met in person. Foremost, I am forever grateful to those wonderful authors of the self-help books that helped me get through difficult times many years ago. I have been a huge believer ever since and have continued to recommend self-help books to many others throughout the years because of my own wonderful experiences.

I would like to thank the Hay House Writer's Community, in particular Reid Tracy and Kelly Notaras, who taught and provided a framework for the whole writing process. This was the most enjoyable learning experience. Thanks also to my fellow writers from the community who provided encouragement along the way. I also want to thank the team at Balboa Press for guiding me through the production, editing and publication process, and getting the job done. It was all very new to me.

To my amazing tribe, Tenille Britten, Elliesha O'Reilly, Dayna Lee and Grace Frances, all who supported me consistently in their own special way over the past two years throughout this writing journey and provided me with honest feedback throughout the revision process. I appreciate you all so much and can't thank you enough. I want to thank my dear friend, Professor Bonnie Barber for your much appreciated feedback. To all my other family, friends and colleagues, thank you for all your encouragement and support over the past two years to keep going and get this book finished.

I want to thank my husband, Shawn Phillips, who supported me through the entire journey and was so patient, putting up with me disappearing into my writing room for several hours on a regular basis at the end of my work day and my days off. More importantly, for providing a haven for me to feel safe and secure in our relationship. Your continued humility, wisdom, unconditional love and acceptance has enabled me to experience what it's like to be myself in a relationship.

I'd also like to acknowledge all my wonderful clients I've had the pleasure of knowing over the years, whose bravery in overcoming difficult relationships has empowered them to find their own happiness. Your collective stories have provided evidence to support the concepts in this book that will help many others in the future.

Finally, it's most important that I acknowledge the inspiration I have received throughout writing this book, which has once again proven to me the existence of a Higher Power. You never disappoint – Thank you… Thank you… Thank you!

INTRODUCTION

This book is written in response to a need that's become evident through more than two decades of my experience as a clinical psychologist. This has mostly come from women, though men also deal with the same kinds of relationship struggles. Substantial heartache on many levels generally follows a relationship breakdown. Many times, people will continue to carry regrets for persevering in a problem relationship long after it ends. Although all individual relationship situations are unique, the same principles apply to most people. This is because there are common principles at work when people find themselves having multiple failed relationships. Some are affected quite severely and decide to give up on relationships altogether. Some comments I've heard throughout my career are, "Why does this keep happening to me?" and further on, "Why don't we know about this stuff?" And many times, after exploring their unique patterns, "You should write a book about this!" So here it is!

Throughout this book, you will be guided through the principles that have us making the same mistakes every time, leaving us bereft, heartbroken, and bewildered that we've ended up in the same situation yet again! Strangely, in many cases, people think they have chosen so differently from previous times and perceive their new partners as being totally opposite from those they've been attracted to in the past. Later, they may recognise a distinct pattern that has repeated itself several times. This book provides detailed, step-by-step strategies to help break those damaging patterns and form new healthier patterns to guide you toward finding what you really want and need in a partner.

Couple relationships generally start during our teens or early adulthood, and sometimes a little later. During this time, we learn about the types of people we're attracted to, and we become aware of certain things that give us that warm feeling on the inside, alerting us to the fact that we are attracted to them. Depending on our experiences, we can either have healthy attractions where things end up working out well, or we can have attractions that are not so healthy, which result in having troubled relationships throughout most of our lives.

Many tears have been shed in my therapy room due to multiple episodes of lost love and long-lost dreams that end up shattered, leaving desperate people not knowing what to do. Some have said, "That's it! I'm staying single!" Or, "I'm just no good at relationships … I give up!" That may seem a reasonable choice, though many of us know deep down—even if we don't want to admit it—that we really want to find that someone special. We want to experience the wonderful feeling that only comes from being in love or having an intimate relationship with someone. To want and need intimacy and that special someone with whom we can share our lives is a natural part of the human condition. When we don't have that, we can find ourselves sometimes secretly searching for that someone. Understandably, some will choose to be alone, especially as we grow older and are more comfortable in our own company.

The major culprit that gets us into problem relationships is unawareness. We have blind spots, lacking insight and understanding about the repeated patterns that show up in our relationships. The problem with blind spots is that while we're caught up in our own little whirlwinds of life, we can carry on without noticing potential pitfalls that may get us into trouble, usually by following what is comfortable and familiar. Then later, we come to a realisation that we could have been doing things differently for most of our lives and been enjoying the benefits of having a happier, more fulfilling life by approaching things in a different way.

There are many variables that contribute to us having relationship blind spots, and throughout this book, I have aimed to cover as many as possible. Most problematic relationships can be avoided from the start if we learn the processes that guide us into making better choices. This means we need to learn how to be discerning. It's not that simple though as we can become ensnared in our own cyclic relationship patterns with unique features, influenced by our personalities and life experiences. Such influences come from our previous relationships, our growing-up experiences in our families of origin, and our unique sense of who we are in the world, otherwise known as our "sense of self."

My intention is to have this message reach as many people as possible. I've aimed to make it easy to follow so that even if you don't see yourself as a great reader, you'll be able to follow, learn the concepts, and do any of the exercises you choose. I believe it's important for us to make our own choices in life. This is how we become empowered. And for this reason, the exercises are presented as invitations rather than instructions. I trust that you'll recognise those things that need your attention.

I share some of my personal experiences that have given me insight into this well-trodden area of failed relationships. Throughout my earlier adult years, I truly believed I was doomed in relationships as I had no guidance or understanding of what makes a relationship work. Then after a major crisis in my life around my early forties, I took a few years to stay free from relationships. During that time, I worked out my own patterns, which helped me to find my way forward. This process enabled me to gradually develop the insights I needed to see myself through my recovery. I read multiple self-help books, which taught me about myself and provided me with the insights I needed to start turning my life around. This enabled me to gain some understanding about my own life journey and to break the negative relationship patterns that had dictated my life. The principles in this book are guided by that same process.

My spiritual journey also played a major role in the journey of my recovery and continues to define who I am in my personality and nature. This has largely contributed to helping me to find my way out of my pattern of harmful relationships. I was acutely aware of the guidance I was receiving at different times as it was always made evident to me. I was also able to see in hindsight how I had betrayed my own gut instincts when I knew certain relationships were not good for me. The divine guidance I received was a major factor in my ability to learn how to be discerning, which is the central feature of this book. Discernment in relationships is the ability to know and understand the difference between what's harmful for us and what's in our best interests, so we can make better choices.

As you follow the procedures in this book, you will learn how to make the shift from acting on your attractions to the wrong people to becoming discerning and discovering the type of person who can bring you happiness. This comes from first developing a healthy sense of self, so you can create healthier connections in your relationships.

You will receive knowledge regarding the patterns that have collectively formed from a combination of experiences from myself and many wonderful people I have worked with over the years. Though all presented with unique issues, the identifiable similar patterns are evident. I address them in a general sense without implicating any particular individuals. They can be applied to anyone who is either starting their relationship journey or has a history of finding themselves in problematic relationships.

The overall message is designed to help the reader learn how to develop a healthy relationship with themselves, become unstuck if in a difficult situation, or improve their current relationship and learn how to create harmony within it. There are also practical implications for improving mental health conditions caused by relationship stress. Those suffering with relationship distress generally present with depression or anxiety and are often referred by their doctor for psychological treatment. This also has future implications for reducing the number of failed relationships that impact significantly on the children who get caught in the middle of family breakups that happen all too often.

This book is written for any adults who are interested in making better choices in their relationships or who are just starting out and need some guidance. It's mostly suitable for readers from twenty to fifty years old, though not exclusively. Older women have presented with similar well-trodden paths, and sadly, some have needed to face their personal regrets about their lifelong patterns of poor relationship choices. Others have found love later in life by learning how to become more discerning and finding a suitable companion.

The information provided is based on many things I've found myself repeatedly saying to people while helping them with their mental health issues and subsequently providing guidance for them in their relationship journeys. I've realised that it's not always easy for people to recognise what's happening to them when they're in the thick of things. I trust you'll embrace these concepts and find the content and insights in this book a valuable contribution and resource to your life both personally and in your relationship journey.

This book is in three parts and for good reason as there are three areas that need a lot of consideration in the process of developing healthy connections in relationships. Although they are separate topics, they are interrelated as they are all necessary components involved in the ability to create and maintain healthy, lasting relationships.

Part 1 is the foundation of this message and is focused on getting your relationship with yourself on track. Believe it or not, this is the most important thing you can do, firstly to secure your own personal happiness, and then to increase the potential for finding a suitable mate. We need to be aware of who we are, of our values and beliefs, and all those things that are important to us in life. There is also the need to develop a genuine appreciation for who we are in the world and to learn the value of love and compassion for ourselves. So, the details are spelled out for you here in a way that provides ample opportunity to see yourself in a more positive way with the intention of building and developing a healthier sense of self.

Part 2 is about your relationship experiences and gives you an opportunity to explore the nature of your patterns, what sorts of people you are attracted to, and how you can develop a deeper understanding and knowledge of how to cultivate good relationships. If you are yet to have a relationship, you will benefit from learning the sound principles involved in starting the process. You'll have a better chance through educating yourself about what you need to help you make healthy choices for your future. If you're already in a relationship, you may benefit from getting back to some of the basics that have the potential to enhance your relationship or alternatively, give you the courage to leave if it's not working for you.

Part 3 addresses sound principles on how to get things working well from the start, so you can increase your chances of creating and keeping a successful relationship. You will learn some of the basics about how to develop your communication skills and nurture a positive mindset toward being in a relationship. This provides you with the opportunity to start things off on the right foot and enhances the potential for maintaining a healthy relationship in the longer term. You will learn how to avoid common damaging situations that cause relationship trauma, which is often difficult to repair. Through these last chapters, you will learn some basic principles about what is needed to get your relationship on track and working harmoniously.

Self-help books have so much to offer for different life situations, and I am their biggest fan! Obviously not everything can be covered within my perspective and focus on the relationship journey presented in this book. Therefore, a reading list is provided for those who would like to explore some areas further.

I hope you enjoy reading this book as much as I have enjoyed writing it!

DISCLAIMERS

All situations in this book are based on general and collective information and do not contain any specific information directed at any individual, couple, or family.

The information in this book is not intended as an alternative to therapy. Should any issue arise that causes distress or highlights unresolved issues, seeking therapy from a qualified professional with expertise in the area of concern is highly recommended.

This book aims to provide insights and does not claim to give full answers to individual problems with which people may identify. Nor does it aim to address complex problems that require professional help.

PART 1
YOUR JOURNEY HAS A BEGINNING

Be committed to the relationship you have with yourself.

We get so committed to other relationships,

but often sort of toss ourselves away.

We get around to ourselves only now and then.

So, really care for who you are.

Be committed to loving yourself.

Take care of your heart and soul.

—Louise Hay, Louise Hay Quotes

CHAPTER 1

IT STARTS WITH YOU

Your relationship with yourself is the basis for all other relationships!

Have you noticed that there are so many quotes about self-love, about taking care of yourself, about guarding your heart and soul? As I was searching for a quote that said what was appropriate for what I wanted to convey to my readers, I became aware that quotes have become so plentiful and forthcoming that we can very easily skip past the meaning of them and take an, "Oh, that's nice," stance without really taking on board what the words actually mean. It became obvious to me that there are different levels of understanding—brief, flippant, feel-good ones, and deeper, more thoughtful interpretations.

I don't consider one better than the other as they are all wonderful and add to the solutions rather than the problems in life in many ways. However, sometimes we need to look into things a little more deeply to get the most out of the meaning of the quote. This certainly applies to Louise Hay's quote that I chose for the first part of this book. When I came across it, I saw its deep relevance to our relationship journey, no matter who we are and no matter what type of relationship we may have in our lives. So, let's go deeper and look at this quote a little more closely.

What does it mean to be committed to the relationship we have with ourselves? Do we even realise that it is a relationship, or do we see ourselves as just being individuals? I believe it is evident through what we understand now, informed by all the modern-day philosophers through the principles and practice of mindfulness meditation, that each of us most definitely do have a relationship with ourselves. For instance, we are now more aware than ever of how we speak to ourselves in our minds, of the strong emotions we project towards ourselves, and the stories we tell ourselves in our heads about what we believe about ourselves in the world. They all support the reality that we do have a relationship with ourselves. It is also evident that we can treat ourselves very poorly at times.

Let's face it, we can be really mean to ourselves at different times and in certain situations. We can judge ourselves harshly over various actions we've taken and thoughts we've had. We can slip into self-protection mode to save face and then beat ourselves up about it later. And we can blow things out of proportion when something upsets us but is not exactly true to our circumstances. How many times have you ruminated on something that happened and spent the rest of the day being angry and giving yourself a hard time because of the blame and shame that's been created? I know I have, and I know a lot of other people do the same thing. People who engage in such thought processes are often suffering with low self-esteem to some extent, sometimes with depression or anxiety, and often with an ongoing struggle regarding their sense of self—that is, how they see themselves as a person.

The good news is that we don't have to be that way, and we certainly don't have to stay that way. I have come to realise that we often underestimate the power of our choices. We can choose to be more compassionate, understanding, and patient with ourselves as we learn to live in a more positive way and embrace our authenticity rather than trying to project an outwardly acceptable image. We can understand that we are human, and because of this fact, we are just like everyone else and will make some mistakes. We are learning more and more through all the wonderful teachers and authors today about how to be kinder to ourselves, to look after ourselves, and to treat ourselves in caring, compassionate ways. We are learning to make better choices in our lives.

Through different therapeutic modalities available and research in the neurosciences, we're learning that we can change the way we look at ourselves and form more positive self-images. This helps us to abandon the negative scripts we've previously taken on about how we see ourselves. In doing this, we are able to create different scripts that help us define who we are, thereby renewing our lives in the process. These are just some of the indicators that prove to us that we do have a relationship with ourselves and that we are not just one-dimensional individuals. We could say "I am." And we could also say, "I am, and I am what I think I am." In this sense, when there is no connection to others, we are still in a close relationship with ourselves. For this reason, it makes a significant difference to whether we see ourselves in a positive or a negative light.

The next part of the quote is about getting so committed to our relationships that we sort of toss ourselves away. How incredible that we would ever do that! Why on earth would we toss ourselves away? Interesting how this quote says, "sort of," as though we do it mindlessly, like an automatic reaction based on some idea that we're not as important as anyone else. This really speaks volumes to me. In my personal life and in my clinical experience, I have found this to be a common phenomenon.

So many people have a different set of rules for themselves than they have for anyone else. For some, there is a tendency to regularly engage in self-criticism, demonstrating through their decisions and actions that they have a serious lack of self-consideration. For those who are more entitled, there is a tendency for self-elevation and lack of consideration for others. Either way, each self-concept is out of balance and can lead to major interpersonal problems in life. Interestingly, these two opposing types can often find themselves discovering each other, which is covered in more detail later.

The part about getting committed to other relationships is about giving so much of ourselves in our relationships to the point that we lose sight of who we are as individuals. Our identities become swallowed up by the shift of focus and energy on to the other person and trying to hold the relationship together. This is usually due to fear of losing that person and being alone. In such cases we may ask, "Why would we lose ourselves for the sake of a relationship?" This is an area that has been well-documented and is often referred to as co-dependency. There have been many books written on the subject, which were primarily and mostly related to the field of addictions, such as alcohol and drugs, but also to relationships themselves—thus called, relationship addiction.

I am saddened to say that this problem is still alive and well to this day. People still lose themselves in their relationships, and this is mainly because they have not developed a stable sense of self. They have lacked the ability to form any solid concept of who they are because they have such little understanding, appreciation, value, or knowledge of themselves. To this day there are many cases in which people prefer to replace any form of self-concept with who they think their partners want them to be. The relationship has become more important than any self-interests, and this requires that the other person in the relationship be given preference to whatever extent is necessary to avoid problems and keep things running smoothly. How tragic, right?

When we deny those things we need in order to be ourselves—to be who we are—and only consider our personal needs in small and limited ways, we're missing out on living the life we are meant to live and in being our authentic selves. We are depleting our energy on pleasing others to the detriment of our own well-being. This has serious implications for how we live our lives. The reason being that energy is like time; we only have a specified amount in a day, and it's important that we put our energy where it's going to matter. If we put all our energy into another person, we deprive ourselves of the energy we may need to meet our own basic needs, including what is required to look after ourselves emotionally, psychologically, and in a practical sense. To maintain good mental health, we need to find a balance in the way we see ourselves in life and allow enough time to give ourselves what we need to meet our own needs and have some left to reach out to others.

A very sobering thought about all this is that we come into this world alone and leave it when our time here on earth is done, usually also alone. We do not come into this world with a mandate to make another person the centre of our lives, neglecting ourselves in the process. Between the time we're born and the time we depart, we develop through our childhood and then have choices to make about how we will live our lives. It's important that we learn how to look after ourselves and consider our needs and how we organise our social world. This includes who we choose to allow into our lives, how we allow ourselves to be treated, and how we treat others. It's all about finding the balance and not allowing ourselves to be more important or less important in our relationships.

Looking after our heart and soul is about having love for ourselves and reaching out in the same way to others. This is the secret to finding true happiness in our relationships; we can only connect authentically with another when we have a secure and solid sense of self. We need to practice self-love, to believe we are lovable, and clear out any obstacles that come in the way of that belief. After all, no one is born feeling unloved. We need to clear the pathway to self-love so we can attract the kind of love that is enduring and gives us what we really need. It is so necessary for all of us to put substantial effort into knowing and loving who we are as a basis for cultivating healthy relationships and especially for finding our life partner, that person we want to have children with and be with throughout our lives.

The following chapters in this section are designed to help you on your journey of developing your relationship with yourself. This is a prerequisite for finding, developing, and keeping a healthy relationship. Whether or not you are already in a relationship, you will benefit from the principles provided in these pages. Initially, the focus needs to address your sense of self as this will enhance your relationships and prevent any future relationship mishaps. Let's now delve into what it means to develop the sense of self.

Optional Exercises

The following suggestions are designed to help you with whatever you see as relevant to your personal circumstances. They are an invitation to engage in whatever processes you choose based on your personal needs.

Things to Ponder

- Am I committed to the relationship I have with myself?
- Do I tend to "toss myself away" when I get into a relationship?
- Do I always maintain my sense of self whether I'm in a relationship or not?
- Am I honest in how I see myself in relationships?
- Do I take care of my heart and soul?
- Do I please others at the expense of looking after myself?

Things I Can Do

- Take notice of my commitment to the relationship I have with myself.
- Reflect on previous or current relationships; commit to valuing my needs and opinions.
- Take notice of my gut instinct with my relationships.
- Take more notice of the things that really feed my soul.

- Take notice when something drains me and feels soul-destroying; action self-care.
- Start a journal of my relationship journey starting with me; this is highly recommended.

CHAPTER 2

SENSE OF SELF

Our perceptions of ourselves influence the quality of all our relationships!

Sense of self covers many aspects of ourselves. It means that we have a perception of who we are in the world, whether we are aware of that or not. It's about all the characteristics that define us, about different aspects of our personalities, and all those things we know that we like and dislike. It also refers to the values we have in life, what we believe in, and the things we are passionate about. Most important, it is about the essence of how we see ourselves as individuals aside from what we achieve in our lifetimes. This means that a healthy sense of self is not about fame, wealth, or status achieved. It's more about who we are within our core beings that define our true authentic selves. This includes having awareness of ourselves in a social context with consideration of others.

Evidence of differences in sense of self is all around us. For instance, we are aware that some people seem to be more fortunate in life than the so-called average person. We also know that some of those people have achieved wealth in their lives or have become famous for their talents, special skills and abilities, or for creating and maintaining a successful business. Those achievements, as wonderful as they are, can only define a part of a person; they do not completely define their inner sense of self. Nor do they satisfy what is most important to satisfy their sense of well-being.

For example, we are often shocked when we hear that someone wealthy or famous, seeming to have everything, has been suffering with depression or another mental health condition, and some who have even taken their own lives. We can't imagine how people who seem so successful could become so desperately unhappy, and especially when they decide to opt out of life. We are deeply saddened to hear about it and are left with a sense of sorrow that can be hard to shake off. Obviously, we don't know about the internal pain those people were suffering or what was happening that was not evident to the outside world. We have to wonder about their internal sense of self and why it didn't provide them the resilience they needed to survive whatever they were facing. It's true that life can be challenging at times, and growing a healthy sense of self allows us to build resilience to face our challenges.

When I talk with someone about his or her sense of self, I am sometimes confronted with a blank stare and a confused or doubtful look. People can be quite surprised by the idea that they actually are expected to have an individual sense of self, to know who they are as a person. Sometimes they are very aware that they don't know who they are and will say so in no uncertain terms. They will also sometimes refer to their achievements as being proof of either having a sense of self or that they have no sense of self because they don't believe they've achieved much in life. I hope we are now all on the same page about this. It is not about achievements, fame, or fortune but about that intrinsic self-understanding of who we are as individuals, complete with an understanding of our values and place in the world with others. What we do with that are expressions of who we are.

The term "sense of self" is used quite a lot in my profession and is often used in our correspondence with medical professionals regarding referrals, so it may seem a little cliché to some. However, I make no apologies for the term because it's at the core of many mental health problems that people struggle with throughout their lives. Having a poor sense of self resides at the base of mood disorders, depression, anxiety disorders, personality disorders, sometimes post-traumatic stress, and often the results of a broken relationship that has left some deep scars. I've heard many psychologists speak of the sense of self when attending seminars, conferences, and workshops. In the mental health field, we have a shared understanding of what this means, and to some level, it is self-explanatory.

First of all, let's look at what it means to have a sense of self. Then we can address what happens when one's sense of self is damaged. Both areas are important in their own rights and worthy of exploration.

You may have heard that famous quote that originated from William Shakespeare: "This above all; to thine own self be true." Way back then, in the sixteenth century, this primal and very important human need somehow came to the bard's attention. Whenever I hear this quote, it makes me think of how important it is to be respectful and honest with ourselves. It can seem so easy at times to sell ourselves out for the sake of pleasing others. But when we do that, we are not being honest or respectful towards ourselves.

When we are busy seeking approval from others or thinking their ideas and advice are always better than our own, we cannot be truly honouring and nurturing our own personal sense of our self. Just because we exist, we owe it to ourselves to be honest and stand in our integrity. We can do this in a way that is respectful to ourselves and to others. In doing so, we don't allow others to take advantage of us as they soon learn to respect us because we respect ourselves, and in turn, this becomes evident to others.

We can't expect other people to know things that concern us better than we know ourselves. In fact, no one knows us more intrinsically than we know ourselves. When our sense of self is lacking, we have a tendency to reach out to others for direction and guidance. In such cases, we are more likely to move away from our own needs to either please another person or avoid making decisions for ourselves because of something lacking in our personal development. This is such an important issue that may challenge us. But it needs to be addressed as it gets in the way of making the right choices for ourselves, including choosing our partners.

When we each take more notice of our inner self and respect our core essence deep within our soul, we will get to know who we really are. It is only you who really knows all those things you are curious about. Only you can truly know what your passions are and those deep desires you have for what you want and need for your life. Only you will understand at a deep level what is needed to find your destiny in this life. Absolutely no one else can do this for us. Other people can be sounding boards or sometimes provide some guidance and direction for our lives, but we need to be responsible for our own decisions and opinions if we want to develop a healthy sense of self.

Your sense of self becomes damaged when you don't believe in yourself, when you ignore your true needs, and fail to give yourself the respect you deserve for just being you. The damage usually comes from early life experiences; it most likely started during childhood or adolescence. It may have then been further reinforced through early adulthood. For instance, we may have grown up feeling worthless or unimportant, and that our needs didn't matter. In adulthood, this may lead to being in an abusive relationship or one that favoured the partner, leaving us feeling even more worthless. Further along the track, we may have struggled with confidence in our own ability to be our authentic selves. By this time, we have more than likely become consumed with excessive negative thoughts and self-talk, creating a damaging belief system that comes from those earlier experiences that sent us all the wrong messages.

Incredibly, this happens so easily and can come from parents, teachers, and other influential people throughout our lives who had the best of intentions and usually thought they were doing the right thing. The messages we derive from those good intentions often create self-doubt in us, along with the tendency to think that others always know better. This can create a very disturbed sense of self that is difficult to shake off, though it lives mostly in our states of unawareness. When we become more aware, we can challenge such negative messages and deal with them in a way that pays respect to ourselves and others involved.

Life can become very confusing when one's sense of self is not intact. It results in poor decision-making—the habit of constantly looking for someone else to make the decisions and to feel increased anxiety when there is a demand for a decision to be made. You will hear people say things like, "What do you think I should do?" Or, "I don't know what to do," sometimes even stated in a tone of panic. The task of making a decision is so difficult because of the lack of confidence in being able to take that risk, which is laden with insecurities that have an underlying fear of getting something wrong. In most cases, there is no right or wrong, just a decision to choose between one thing or another.

We don't often hear a very self-assured, confident person say things like that. There is generally more of a calm, thoughtful response when faced with decisions, especially when they relate to difficult life issues. That doesn't necessarily mean they will have the answers. It just means they are confident enough to know they will be able to sort things out, and if they don't have the answers now, the answers will come to them at some point. They will not perceive any need to panic, turn it into a drama, or get hugely stressed about it. They will even have no qualms about saying they'll think about things if that's what is required, and some time is needed for a little more thought.

This doesn't mean we should never listen to anyone else or that we should dismiss any of their opinions. We all have opinions, and others can sometimes have great ideas and offer helpful advice about things that affect us and our lives. This is especially true if they have expertise in a certain area, and we can really benefit from their knowledge. However, at the end of the day, it is important that we learn to make our own decisions about those things that are concerning us and will impact our lives. Most decisions are not about life-or-death situations, and we can sometimes change our minds later. In the meantime, we can go with what we choose and make the most of it.

If you are reading this and thinking, *But that's who I am. I am indecisive. I've always been that way. I am really bad at making decisions for myself. I always need others to help me out with things; I can never do that on my own.* The good news is that you were not born indecisive, so you don't have to continue believing that you are. There is no such thing as an indecisive gene! It was something you learned along the way, and you can just as easily learn another way to deal with this issue. Your next decision can be to work on developing your ability to make decisions for yourself, thereby overcoming the habit of depending too much on the opinions of others to guide you through your life.

A good start to overcoming this problem is to begin doing regular mindfulness meditations to help you learn how to quiet your mind and go deeper within yourself. This is the place where the seed of your sense of self resides. Tap into it; nurture it. Imagine it's like a seed that's just sprouted and needs nurturing with attention and focus. This is what is required to get the real benefit out of mindfulness meditation. It requires a stillness in which you can just be to give yourself that time and allow that space so you can receive inner peace and guidance. That is what really works. Then start doing things differently. Be more aware of your abilities and the endless possibilities rather than focusing on what you can't do.

Another thing you can do to strengthen your sense of self is to allow yourself to start thinking about your personal passions and desires. Ask yourself, "What am I passionate about?" Or, "Where does my curiosity take me?" or, "What would I really love to do?" I ask many people this, and most times, they will say they don't know. It's fine to not know, but what is important to know is that great benefits can be gained by just asking the question. This starts the process that can continue until it leads you to finding those things that feed your soul, so it's worth keeping on your radar. What comes from within you helps to develop and nurture your sense of self.

When you are being yourself and engaging in the things you truly love from the depth of your heart, you will know what it means to feed your soul. You will also become more confident in your ability to make decisions for your life. And will have gained a healthier sense of self. This skill of independent thinking is necessary for enabling us to have healthy relationships throughout our lives, and we develop it further through interacting with others. We speak our truths and are okay if they are different truths than what others hold. Our unique differences are to be valued!

Optional Exercises

These exercises will help you to reflect on your sense of self and encourage you to explore areas that may need some work. The last suggestion is an exercise that has great merit, and I recommend everyone does this one. As you work through this book, you'll see how this relates to learning how to make better choices in your relationships.

Things to Ponder

- What do I know about my sense of self?
- Would I describe my sense of self as healthy?
- Are there some things I need to work on?
- Do I rely on others too much?
- How confident do I feel in taking important steps in my life?
- Do I trust my internal understanding of myself?

Things I Can Do

- Write down my reflections from this chapter in my journal, and set some goals for myself.
- Start writing a full description of myself in my journal, starting with, "I am." You can add to this at any time, so keep it where you can find it easily. You'll need this for an important exercise later in the book. Please note that some people find this exercise rather difficult, especially if they struggle with their self-esteem. If this relates to you, ask for some input from one or two people who know you well and whose opinion(s) you trust. You may get some surprises about what others see in you that you don't see in yourself.

CHAPTER 3

AUTHENTIC SELF-LOVE

Authentic self-love is not vain or selfish but reflects unconditional self-acceptance.

Many people struggle with the concept of self-love. This is especially a challenge for those who suffer with low self-esteem. They are likely to consider self-love as being vain and self-centred, so they go out of the way to avoid any tendency towards anything that is self-focused. I am constantly surprised at how common this misconception is, even though it's something I struggled with myself for many years of my earlier life. Low self-esteem is an inner sense of unworthiness that causes us to see ourselves as being inadequate and unworthy of love from anyone—let alone ourselves. When we suffer with low self-esteem, we generally don't feel too comfortable talking about self-love, so it can be a case of silent suffering with a mindset that perceives ourselves as unacceptable and flawed. Others can easily miss this and have no idea of how we think about ourselves.

Our capacity for self-love does not always seem to be consistent with our ability to love other people, especially those who are our nearest and dearest. Loving others seems to be a whole lot easier for some people. We have loving hearts towards those special people in our lives, family members, close friends, and even those friends we only see occasionally. When we think of them, it comes easy for us to send loving thoughts their way. We feel the connection and want to keep the relationships going. We love to see them, and when we're not with them, we keep a loving attitude towards them, looking forward to seeing them again. They may even provide us with something we perceive that we need in life.

However, when it comes to having those loving thoughts towards ourselves, it often doesn't come so easily. We can really struggle sometimes to see ourselves as being lovable, and this can present a huge imbalance between our perceptions of ourselves and others. Instead of acknowledging and accepting those loving thoughts towards ourselves, we can be too focused on our faults and flaws. Our attention can be so fixed on the things we don't like about ourselves that it becomes the only way we see ourselves. We can fail to notice our own goodness and uniqueness that makes us lovable. We can then struggle to consider that we may be just as lovable as all the other people we see as totally lovable. If we really think about it, is it really okay to have a different set of rules for everyone else than what we have for ourselves? This may seem like a silly question as the answer is evident, though this is the habit many of us have developed in the way we see ourselves in the world.

You may be reading this and realise that it resonates with you; it describes how you feel about yourself. If you can identify with any indicators of not being comfortable with self-love, you may need to give this area a whole lot of attention. A good way of starting to explore this is to check out your self-thoughts and your self-talk. The things we think and say to ourselves in our heads can be quite harsh sometimes, especially when we've made mistakes. We can momentarily lose sight of the fact that we all make mistakes. We know that this is something that makes us human rather than bad or a failure. Yet we can make up mean stories to tell ourselves in our heads that confirm to us that we are unlovable. This will often happen when we have a strong inner critic, which can do a whole lot of damage to our self-esteem. Those things we say to ourselves in our heads are vitally important to our mental health and can make or break us at different times.

Interestingly, we're not always aware that our self-image can also sometimes be quite apparent to others, especially those who are more intuitive than most. We can show several signs that give it away, such as facial expressions, body language, posture, actions, the way we talk about ourselves, and sometimes by the things we don't say about ourselves. You may be surprised to hear that others often feel very uncomfortable when they hear someone give off negative vibes about himself or herself that demonstrate a poor sense of self. It can cause them to pull away and disengage from us, which is often the exact opposite of what we really want.

Another way that demonstrates poor self-esteem is when we do the opposite and boost ourselves up more than we should to help us feel better about ourselves, making us appear superior to others. Often people who do this carry a huge sense of inadequacy, and the behaviour is an overcompensation for how they really feel about themselves. If we scratch beneath the surface in such cases, we are likely to find just as much difficulty in self-love as those who show their inadequacies outwardly. Therefore, appearances may be deceiving in some cases. Either way, there is a need to develop a healthy authentic love towards ourselves.

Addressing the concept of self-love with people can be interesting. A common phrase I hear from people is, "That's just the way I am. I just see myself in a negative way." Other comments I've heard are, "I don't believe I am lovable. I've done too many bad things," or, "I wasn't raised that way. Our family doesn't show love or affection." Some people even talk about being scolded for thinking too highly of themselves while growing up. I have heard numerous people say they were told, "Don't you get too big for your britches!" Such experiences in childhood can be so damaging to our concepts of self-esteem and put us off track from finding a healthy love and appreciation for ourselves.

The good news is that we can change this! We don't have to hold on to those negative ideals, even if we've had them for a long time. We were not born that way. The evidence of this is clear when we take notice of babies and toddlers. They are just little love magnets, relying on their caregivers and expecting as much love as they get without any signs whatsoever of feeling unlovable or having low self-esteem. This is because we didn't come into this world believing we were of no value. And we certainly were not born with negative self-views, so they cannot be a part of our true authentic selves. If we've learned self-loathing, we've done so over many years of wrong thinking about ourselves, and like many other things, we can change that and do things differently.

Many have developed poor self-love from growing up and clinging onto the wrong messages. For instance, if we were chastised for making mistakes or for doing something wrong as children, whether we meant to or not, we may have internalised this by seeing ourselves as "bad" children. We may have even been wrongly told by adults that we were bad when we may have been misbehaving. It only takes for this pattern to be repeated a few times before the belief of, "I am bad" takes root and begins to reflect that self-perception. This has the potential to work against any sense of self-love we acquired in the beginning. It comes from clueless behaviour generated by well-intended caregivers in our pasts who had no idea that their practices caused such damage. On a positive note, I like to think we're getting better at being more psychologically minded in more recent generations.

This poses the question of how we unravel this life-defeating perception of ourselves that causes obstacles in our abilities to practice self-love. Thankfully, we are now aware that the brain is not as hardwired as was believed just a few decades ago. We now know through research and studies in neuroscience and the discovery of neuroplasticity that the brain is malleable (not fixed), and neural pathways can be altered over time by introducing and practicing new ways of thinking and by learning new habits. This means that any wrong thinking previously wired into our brains since childhood and reinforced through years of practice can be altered by how we think and what we do.

New neural pathways can form as we practice more positive ways of thinking and take on new habits. We can do this by recognising the harm negative thoughts do to us and then introducing good thinking practices into our personal worlds. This is especially important when it comes to building self-esteem and learning about how to love and appreciate ourselves in authentic ways that neither put us down nor inflate any false sense of self-importance, which is reactive rather than authentic.

At this point, it's important to mention that this is not about blaming our parents or anyone else who may have caused or contributed to the problem. No one is perfect; everyone makes mistakes, including parents and teachers. Anyone who is a parent with grown children, if they're honest, will tell you that they regret some of the parenting decisions they made. This is completely normal and will be the same for the rising generations of parents. Blaming others is never helpful as it causes us to hold on to resentment and negativity, so this is not about blame. It is, however, about learning to understand ourselves and why we think, feel, and act the way we do. By exploring this, we have the opportunity to identify the negative thoughts we've acquired about ourselves. We are then able to put our energy into challenging and changing our self-view.

First, before we can make those necessary changes, we need to believe that this is something that we can do. Second, we need to identify and ditch those negative beliefs about ourselves. We need to let go of them. All of them! See them as intruders to our sense of self and personal growth. If our negative self-views have dominated our thoughts throughout our lives, we can confidently take a strong position regarding this and state clearly that it must end now! And third, we need to replace negative self-talk and self-beliefs with positive alternatives. There are many positive affirmations available through the internet and in books and other writings to help you along the way, and you will know what you need.

If this resonates with you, take a moment to sit quietly, and access your emotional memory to search and ask yourself where you may have learned that you were unlovable. You may have received messages throughout your childhood that you ought not to have a big opinion of yourself. Or you could have just been so focused on what you did wrong or what you didn't like about yourself that you didn't see the good stuff. You may have been raised in a family that was not able to provide a nurturing, loving environment, so you were not able to differentiate between the person—who was inherently good—from the mistakes, which are part of being human. You may have also received some wrong messages in your earlier adult years through being involved in one or more toxic relationships that reinforced the notion that you were unlovable.

You may find it helpful to recall the things you say to yourself in your mind, and find a positive replacement word for everything you say. For example, instead of thinking, *I'm such an idiot,* you may prefer to think, *I'm learning and growing all the time.* Rather than seeing your mistakes as reflections of being bad, you may try thinking, *I make mistakes because I am human, and I am still lovable regardless!* Instead of thinking, *I'm not very nice looking,* you could replace it with, *Beauty comes from within, and I'm learning to appreciate myself and accept myself the way I am.* You get the idea. Make up your own list. Make it personal. If you want, you can put it up somewhere so you can see it every day to remind you. Over time, your mind will learn to accept the revised scripts you have written for yourself. You will accept and totally believe the truth—that you are lovable—and this will be in the most authentic way.

Optional Exercises

These exercises will help you in your journey as you learn how to develop an authentic, real, and deep love for yourself at your soul level. It is not vain or conceited. Rather, it is an important foundation in order to develop healthy relationships.

Things to Ponder

- How lovable do I see myself?
- What thoughts do I have about myself?
- Where and when did I learn those thoughts?
- What are the stories I make up about myself?
- Have I taken on board everything I need to know and apply from this chapter?
- How can I apply the principles in this chapter to my situation?
- Is this something I noticed in the past about myself and then dismissed it?

Things I Can Do

- Develop my own unique positive affirmations I can say to myself.
- Make some flash cards while I'm learning, and put them where I can see them.

- Practice mindfulness meditation and remember to practice self-love. (Note: This can be done by always approaching yourself with kindness and compassion while meditating. Think of yourself as a vulnerable child who needs nurturing and loving, and give that to yourself.

CHAPTER 4

LOOKING AFTER YOURSELF

Learn to be your own best friend; care for yourself as you do for those you love most!

As you've been learning about getting to know and develop your sense of self and learning how to be your authentic self, we can now move to the area of self-care. In other words, looking after yourself.

First of all, let me ask the question, "What does this mean to you?" It's interesting that people tend to differ in their interpretations of what it means to look after themselves. Some see it as being immersed in meditation, spiritual interests, or engaging in a range of wonderful meditative practices. Others see it as keeping up appearances, making sure they look good, wear the best clothing, use the best cosmetics and perfumes, and, of course, the shoes! Another common perspective of looking after yourself is about financial independence, about working hard and earning a good income, and securing a financial future. Then there are those who are more focused on their physical well-being by engaging in regular exercise and educating themselves about their diets and making sure they keep up with what's good for you in the field of nutrition. So, as we can see there are many themes of what "looking after yourself" means to different people.

Looking after ourselves does not discount any of these approaches to self-care. In fact, truly looking after ourselves means to look after all aspects of our lives. It means creating the right balance so that we can enjoy all areas of our lives while we look after our health and well-being in all those ways. The one thing that is common among almost everyone who has sought therapy with me is that their lives are in some way out of balance. There is generally a lack of clear boundaries, which always involves too much of something and not enough of other things. I am no exception to the rule. I have to work at keeping a healthy life balance. It's always on my radar!

We all live in a very busy world these days, and most of us have to work hard to make ends meet. Many go to work in the morning and come home late, often too tired to do anything but eat, sleep, and get up the next morning to do it all again. That doesn't leave much time for anything else. We're often challenged when we live at such a fast pace to create the balance we really need. Sometimes we only have the weekends to do other things. Even then, the chores are piled up, and we get to Monday with yet another week gone without spending time doing those things we love to do. We're left feeling exhausted and empty at the same time as we haven't given ourselves what we need to re-energise and fill our tanks with the goodness of engaging in the things we love and feel passionate about.

In my experience, overworking seems to be the biggest culprit in creating imbalances in people's lives. It seems so easy to get caught up in the "overworking trap" with large organisations and busy companies placing huge demands on their employees. It's all about getting the job done, often with inadequate staffing and no regard given to the consequences of employees. I've seen many people get caught up in such a trap and always with consequences to the detriment of themselves, their families, and their lifestyles. Very subtly, cracks start appearing in the relationships between partners, children, and entire families. Those cracks turn into problems that can tear relationships apart and leave people feeling lost and vulnerable, sometimes leading to families and couples breaking down altogether. Our relationships with our families and friends are so important and need our time, attention, and nurturance to stay healthy and survive.

Something I do regularly with my clients who are stressed and overextended in their lives, often with relationship problems, is to draw a pie chart for them. I divide it into three with the number 8 in each piece of the pie. The whole pie represents the twenty-four hours in a day. The number 8 in each section represents the allocated time we have for each prescribed daily need. In most cases, we should have about eight hours sleep, give or take a bit depending on individual needs. We generally work for about eight hours, if we're not overdoing it and are keeping reasonable work hours. The biggest shock comes when we see that we have just eight hours left to do everything else. This includes getting ourselves ready for the day, preparing and having meals, getting to and from work, looking after children if necessary, looking after our relationships, dealing with challenges as they appear in our lives—basically everything outside of sleep and work. Thank goodness for weekends! At least then we have a breather to be able to fill in some of those gaps and engage in those other things, such as hobbies and interests. They are the things that feed our soul!

There has never been a more important and challenging time than now for us to find a balance in our lives that meets our needs for self-care. Most of us have so much to fit in to our lives, and we often wish the days were longer. We all need to have some kind of social life. If single, we need time with our families and friends; if in a relationship, we need quality time to spend with our partners. We need to find ways of connecting and developing bonds with our loved ones. And all these relationships need to be maintained.

The connections we have with others are vitally important to our well-being and provide us with a sense of belonging that is not just about what we do for a living. It is a primal need we have as social human beings. Apart from our immediate families, we have extended families and friends who make up our social world. We also have our own personal interests that are important for our personal growth, such as our ability to be creative and engage in things that bring us joy and happiness. We also need downtime to just relax, do whatever we want, having space to ponder about what's going on for us and be able to dream about our goals.

It's fabulous to have a special interest you love to do every chance you get. It could be a sport, playing chess, reading, learning pottery, pushing paint around a canvas, or sketching and learning new art techniques. It could be about writing, whether you're an aspiring author or love to doodle and write poetry or in journals. Different things are important to different people, so having a special area of focus in our lives can be so rewarding, especially if it's something we love. We get great satisfaction from pursuing those things we love to spend our time doing, especially if we're talented and produce a fabulous product. Sadly, this is the very thing that usually gets left off our list of things to do as the demands of life increase for whatever reason, whether it be work or our growing families with all the little added extras that demand our attention. This is especially difficult for single parents, so they may need extra support to pursue their own interests.

Looking after ourselves properly generally requires good planning and self-discipline. A good way to start with a plan is to make a list of all the things you need to do. Include everything that puts demands on your time on a regular basis, such as work, house chores, gardening, and grocery shopping. Then write down the other things that you would like to have in your life, those things that get left out. Once you have a good idea of what you need and want to do, draw up a planner or a calendar for the whole week, and carve out the time when you'll be busy doing those things that you must do. You'll then be able to see what time you have left and where you can fit in some of the things you want to do. You may even need to do some rearranging for this one. It will also show up if you're putting too much time into one thing, like overworking.

This is more challenging, of course, if you have a family as you have more agendas with people's commitments to accommodate. In such cases, you could make planning a family activity to make sure everyone has some time for themselves to do what they enjoy. You may even get to plan date nights to keep your romance going if you are in a relationship. Most of the time, we don't get to do the things we really want to do because we fail to plan and make some space for them. We may feel too tired, busy, or so caught up in doing things for everyone else that we leave no time for what we really need for ourselves. If we continue to do this, we won't feel fulfilled in our lives. When we allow time to do the things we love, we have way more energy to do the more mundane things, and we'll enjoy life more in the process.

I hope by now you have a better understanding of how and why we all need to learn how to look after ourselves. Some people will be challenged by this area and may wonder how on earth they will fit in those things that enable them to take better care of themselves.

And I get it! It's a challenge! However, it's one that needs attention as it has the potential to prevent burnout with work, enhance all our relationships, and is beneficial for our mental health. I also encourage parents to provide good role models for their children by showing them how they can look after themselves as well as being their parents. When children are educated about the needs of others as well as themselves, it instils a sense of empathy in them and becomes a positive part of their childhood experiences, improving their overall education and training.

A final note on this matter is to consider any needs you may have to address for your mental health needs. If you are struggling and could do with a bit of help to sort things out, don't be afraid to seek counselling to help you make the improvements you need to your life. This is an important consideration in looking after yourself and should not be neglected. If it feels uncomfortable to address this area, the most likely reason is that you're not accustomed to self-care. As I say to many people in such situations, you need to get out of your comfort zone and become more comfortable with what is unfamiliar. This is how positive changes can start to take place and bring about the desired outcome. You are worthy of self-care!

Optional Exercises

The following suggestions will prompt you to look at your life balance and help you to develop some planning, make some changes, and reorganise your life where necessary.

Things to Ponder

- Do I put too much energy into one thing in my life?
- Do I spend too much time working?
- Do I allow enough time for the people who are important to me?
- Do I engage in the things I am passionate about?
- What are the things that I love to do? Do I make time for them?
- Do I make excuses about being too busy to do things for myself?

Things I Can Do

- Map on a pie chart where I spend time on my average day.
- Identify the imbalances in my lifestyle.
- Identify what changes need to happen to develop a better life balance.

- Pay attention to my lifestyle, and monitor it to see what changes are needed.
- Acknowledge and address the things I have been neglecting.
- Get a planner to map out when I can fit in time for my own needs.
- Write my reflections regarding self-care in my journal.
- Seek professional help if I am struggling to take care of myself.

CHAPTER 5

SELF-CONSIDERATION

You are just as important and worthy of consideration as anyone else!

Self-consideration is generally lacking in people who tend to sacrifice their own needs for the sakes of others. Some are identified as excessively doing things for others without paying attention to their own needs. People may say such things as, "You're always taking care of everyone else! You don't seem to get too much time for yourself, do you?" Comments like these can come from different sources yet go unheard as though the words are meaningless. They could be disregarded because there's no real connection to attending to their own needs. The comments may even cause a level of discomfort. Some people gain a lot of satisfaction from doing things for others and get carried away, forgetting about their own needs. Alternatively, they may have grown up not being allowed to consider their own needs. I've even heard people say, "I don't deserve it." Ouch! It really cuts to the core to hear someone say that. And it is a clear indication that this issue needs some serious attention.

Self-consideration is an essential prerequisite to forming happy and healthy relationships with others. Getting our head around what this really means will help us to better understand how it plays out in our minds and in our lives. It's also important to be more aware if we have issues with forming healthy relationships, so we can work on developing healthier ones. Self-consideration is an expression of self-care, which then becomes noticeable to others. It influences how we interact with others in our social settings with partners, families, and friends. For example, we learn how to give and take, behaving in ways that promote fairness in our daily living. Without this skill, people can be taken advantage of by those who are more entitled—or at least those who feel more entitled. This is not always obvious but can become more evident as the relationship progresses and preferences appear to consistently sway in favour of the same person.

Many people have blind spots regarding this issue. Those who lack self-consideration and consistently show preferences to everyone else without considering their own needs, can suffer in silence for a long time. After reading the previous chapter about self-care, can you guess what the problem is and what may be missing here? I'm sure you're getting the gist of this issue and have guessed correctly. It is, of course, balance! Our social interactions and relationships need to be balanced, and it's all about genuine giving and receiving. We need to be aware of how much we give of ourselves to others, and make sure we're considering our needs in the process. Whether it's about how much we share of ourselves personally or how we extend ourselves in more practical ways, we would do well to instil and maintain a healthy balance in our relationships.

Of course, it's not wrong to give of ourselves to others. That's a great thing to do and so necessary in this largely self-centred world. Some of us have family members and others who are close to us that sometimes need caring for, so this is an important consideration. After having a mother with physical disabilities for many years, I really appreciate those amazing people who helped her in many ways. However, this is not about helping those in need. It's more about what we do in our regular, day-to-day relationships, and whether we also consider our own needs. Whether or not we have the responsibilities of taking care of others, we also need to take time out to care for ourselves. For example, if we have extra responsibilities with family members that take up a lot of our time and energy, we will benefit from ensuring we also consider our own needs in the grand scheme of things.

Lack of self-consideration has been identified as being associated with the tendency for people to be overly responsible. This refers to those who take responsibility for people in their lives that goes way beyond the call of duty. It's generally an automatic response that aims to fill the needs of others. It can also have the underlying current of needing to feel adequate or accepted. Sometimes it's the only thing that makes people feel worthwhile, so they must continue giving to feel good about themselves. This generally arises from the way life shaped them through their experiences in their families of origin. They became accustomed to being that way in their earlier lives with little or no opportunity for meeting their own needs. So then, guess what happens when they get into relationships? I'm sure you're a step ahead of me here and will recognise that if you are the one doing all the giving, you will be a sitting duck for a partner prepared to do all the taking.

Once in a committed relationship, if things are out of balance in this way, it can become very tiresome and cause problems. This will come up regularly in couple therapy situations as it's often at the top of one of the partner's list of gripes. They will comment on how their relationship is too one-sided in favour of their partner. They may say how they're fed up with having to do everything in the house, while their partner is loafing about, not getting any help or support from them, or about anything else where they feel they're doing most of the work. When confronted, those doing the taking often remain completely oblivious and can become defensive. They may respond by either finding unrelated things to throw back at their accusing partner, be highly offended by the accusations and become haughty, or they may become quiet, as though they're hearing it for the first time. When we practice self-consideration, we give clear messages about how we expect others to treat us, and it's important to convey this message early in the relationship.

The tendency to constantly look out for everyone else to the extent of discounting and neglecting our own needs is a pattern based on our beliefs about ourselves in the world, reflecting an attitude that we consider everyone else more important than ourselves. In therapy, the term "self-sacrificing" is sometimes used to describe this pattern of behaviour. It is more common in those who have low self-esteem or a poor sense of self and consistently give preference in consideration towards partners or friends. There are multiple features associated with this self-sacrificing behaviour and reasons for its presence. They often include fear of rejection or of not being accepted and present as people pleasing. The main principle at work is that the person always acts in a way that favours the other.

Although we may have learned this early in life, this belief is not based on truth. Neither is it fair or of any real value to the one who gives too much, nor to the one who takes too much. It breeds inadequate self-consideration for one partner and entitlement in the other that, if not addressed, can intensify the problem over time. The self-sacrificing partner can eventually become resentful, while the entitled partner is likely to become even more entitled and self-absorbed than before. Other people do matter. They do! However, it's not good for either partner when the relationship is one-sided. If you recognise this as being an issue, you may want to address your personal situation.

Finding and maintaining a balance in our approaches to

relationships are key to avoiding getting into a self-sacrificing and entitlement pattern. If you're reading this and already in a relationship that is lacking equality, all is not lost! You can address this by doing some reflection, talking it over with your partner, and constructing a plan to make some necessary changes. You could decide how to approach the problem together, and if necessary, get some couple's therapy to help sort it out. You could also do some reading on how to develop a healthy relationship and make a commitment to start doing things differently.

One common factor amongst self-sacrificing people is that sometimes there's an obstacle with the thought of changing that habit. That is, the very thought of considering their own needs causes them to think they're being selfish. Many people wrongly interpret self-care or self-consideration as being selfish. People say things like, "Wouldn't that make me really selfish?" or, "I don't want to be selfish." I can't tell you how many times I have heard these kinds of statements, and this belief can be an obstacle to change. Changing this false perception needs to include becoming accustomed to believing and thinking a certain way about this, and to think differently feels really uncomfortable. It's the kind of thinking that is interpreted as, "Giving is the right thing to do," and, "Any consideration towards yourself is selfish." Remember that we sometimes need to question ourselves when we see we have a different set of rules for ourselves than there are for others.

The question you can ask yourself is, "Where did I learn this, and how did I get to think I don't deserve the same as others?" Then, "How can I break this demeaning habit?" You became that way from a belief system that probably started early in life and was reinforced by many years of practice. This could have come through parental role modelling with one overly accommodating parent and the other being overly entitled. You may have experienced neglect without your needs being considered. You may have grown up in a large family and had to give in to everyone else's preferences, or it could have been for a whole range of other reasons. By recognising where it comes from and understanding that it somehow took us way out of balance, we can gradually start to heal this part of ourselves. We can validate ourselves by knowing how we came to be that way and give ourselves permission to grasp hold of the opportunity to change this self-sabotaging habit.

Just a reminder here that when contemplating this and revisiting your childhood experiences, be sure not to get into blaming anyone, especially your parents. This will only create a victim mentality in yourself that will not be working in your best interests. You can read more about this in following chapters, but for now, just realise that everyone has their story. This is not about fault-finding or blaming but about gaining insights to help you understand yourself better, so you can make the positive changes necessary to make better choices and have a happier life.

If this lack of self-consideration is something you recognise, and you've accepted the message that your needs don't matter, you may benefit from some reflection time to identify how you may have received those messages. This sometimes works better when you're in a meditative state as that's a space where insights can emerge more readily. Once you've identified the source, just see it for what it is with an attitude of acceptance. Again, resist temptation to blame someone. Instead, turn your attention to some of your own needs and how they also matter. Notice the effect that being a self-sacrificing person has had on your life, and make a commitment to embrace the concept of self-consideration.

You may ask, "How do I make the changes?" First, the way we think of ourselves, realising that we have the same rights as everyone else in the world, and they deserve consideration, so we do too. Second, what we say is important, either to ourselves or to others regarding our self-perceptions. Get into the habit of saying to yourself, "I am just as important as everyone else, and everyone is just as important as I am." By doing this, you'll change the way you perceive yourself and how you treat yourself. You can also form your own positive affirmations. The aim? To shift your belief from «I don't matter," to "I matter just as much as everyone else!" The evidence of living a fairer life with consideration to yourself and others will follow.

Optional Exercises

These exercises will help you to identify your level of self-consideration, about how much you treat yourself similarly to others, and to what extent you consider your own needs. It may also challenge and help those who are more entitled and lack consideration for others.

Things to Ponder

- Do I consider my own needs as well as those of others?
- How much do I accommodate others without considering my own needs?
- How much discomfort do I feel when considering my own needs?
- Do I have a balance in the way I think of myself in relation to others?
- Do I think too little or too much of myself?
- What evidence do I have in how balanced I am in my approach to my relationships?

Things I Can Do

- Work out some positive affirmations I can say to myself on a regular daily basis.

- Monitor my thoughts and actions about how much I practice healthy self-consideration.
- Recognise any imbalances in my relationships, and make any necessary changes.
- Notice any discomfort I experience with practising self-consideration.
- Embrace any discomfort necessary in making the changes.

CHAPTER 6

ALLOWING FOR GROWTH

We are continuously evolving and growing throughout our lives!

Many of us have gone through incredible hardships in life. If we talk to someone long enough and get to know him or her a little, we'll realise there is always more to the person than meets the eye. Whether they've been through earlier traumas or had reasonably smooth lives, there are always things we can learn from others. In the same manner, others can learn from us, especially when we're willing to share some of our experiences. A certain openness and vulnerability are necessary for us to be able to connect with each other at a deeper level, so we can learn from each other and consequently develop our personal growth. We learn much about ourselves through our interactions with others, from reading books, watching shows, through our work and hobbies, and our personal thoughts. We gain further understanding of ourselves through opportunities to hear stories and ideas we can relate to, connect with, and from which we can learn life lessons.

People who seek therapy differ greatly in their ability or willingness to look at things differently, mainly because it means there's something they need to change. Personal growth requires change. It sounds ridiculously simple and yet makes so much sense. If we don't change anything, things remain the same, and we have no means by which we can grow. We deny ourselves the opportunity to make positive changes in our lives that will make our lives better. We can get caught up and become stuck in difficult situations that lead us to feeling trapped, miserable, and depressed. At times we can even lose hope of ever being able to get out of the bad situations we are in or the unhelpful habits we've formed by giving into them and consequently having them rule our lives. The problem is that we don't usually stop and think about all this. We just kind of morph into doing more of the same thing day after day, often making the same mistakes and then, on reflection, can become regretful. We can even get into the habit of chastising ourselves.

To overcome this debilitating habit, a certain amount of brutal honesty with ourselves is required. I went to a women's retreat many years ago that was led by a wise woman who spoke about empowerment and motivation. One thing she said that I have never forgotten is, "Why is it of so much importance to be right all the time?" She had obviously given this a lot of thought and knew it would have an impact. You could hear a pin drop in the audience of a whole lot of normal chatty women. What she said was absolutely true, and it still is to this day. The need to be right can be an obstacle to our personal growth. It's not as if being wrong about something makes us bad; it doesn't. But we seem to act like it does at times. It's really okay to be wrong sometimes.

This revelation exposed a bad habit of mine that I recognised at the time and have come to realise that it doesn't necessarily go away in a hurry. When we humble ourselves, we can become aware that our shortcomings provide opportunities for change. As we become aware of our reactions in social situations, we can address the issues and work out how we can do things differently in the future. I think it's a brilliant question, and one that we can keep in the back of our minds throughout our lives, especially when it comes to being stubborn about our own points of views, clinging to them like it was a matter of life and death. It hardly ever is! Allowing ourselves to be vulnerable and yes, being wrong sometimes, is necessary if we really want to develop and grow in our personal lives.

If this is ringing true for you as it did for me, it may provide an opportunity for some valuable personal growth. It's true that we can't always be right, because sometimes we do get things wrong. When we take a close look, it really doesn't matter about being right; that only serves to feed our egos. The fact is we are all right sometimes, and we are all wrong sometimes. Isn't that closer to the truth? When you're next in a situation where you really want to express your need to be right, perhaps you could stop and think about how important that issue is and whether there is another angle. You could think about where the other person is coming from and what you may learn from someone on the opposite side of the conversation. This is where personal growth can really start to emerge, when we dare to listen to what others have to say and humble ourselves enough to really listen.

There's something about showing humility that makes others feel comfortable and accepted for who they are. There's no need to pretend to know more than they do and if we're doing this, it may be more about feeling the need to be noticed or accepted in that situation. A healthier way to view such situations is to remember our equality; we are no better or worse than anyone else. This is such an important part of our personal growth. You can put this to the test and see for yourself. Not only is it humbling, it is also insightfully liberating as it is often accompanied with a sense of maturity at having taken responsibility for ourselves.

If you can imagine you're in a relationship with someone you've fallen in love with and you haven't overcome this need to be right all the time, what do you think will happen? What's that habit going to do to your relationship? Chances are your mate may also have the same habit as it's a common habit that seems to affect us all at one time or another. How do you think that will work itself out? By now, hopefully you will either have past experiences spring to mind or if you are new at relationships, you will get the idea that there would be horns locking. Interestingly, arguments are often about trivial things that carry little or no importance. I've seen this play itself out in couple's therapy many times. If it works out well, partners each choose to eat a little humble pie as they realise the consequences of both needing to be right.

Self-reflection is essential to personal growth. If we don't take a step back and have a look in our own backyards, it's going to be far more difficult as we take these troublesome habits into our relationships. The example of needing to be right is just one of many habits that are common in relationships, and they will have an adverse effect on us if we don't give them attention. We can all be stubborn and want our own way, to have our say, and expect others to agree with us or identify with us on some level. If we don't get that feedback, we can act defensively in undesirable ways that can lead to further conflict.

When we attend to our personal growth needs before we get into relationships, we have an opportunity to develop the maturity needed to give us a better start. However, it's never too late. If you're reading this and already in a relationship, recognising issues you may need to address, then take the time to reflect and make any necessary changes. You can then evaluate the outcome and see what difference that makes. This doesn't mean you become a pushover by letting others dominate your opinions. Rather, you may get to agree to disagree. All this, of course, depends on the situation. You can start practicing doing differently those things you identify as being problematic.

Personal growth is a wonderful thing, but it certainly requires our attention. It doesn't usually just happen but will often eventuate following hardship, and often after a relationship breakup. Couples can start off with all the right intentions and later get themselves into an absolute mess in their relationship for many reasons. One of those reasons is when either or both partners do not want to give in to something but expect everything to go their way. News flash! That's not going to amount to a healthy relationship. It will either become a one-sided relationship or it will end. There is no other option. Therefore, attending to our issues and putting time and energy into our personal growth have tremendous preventative qualities and will hold us in good stead as we travel through on our relationship journey.

Sometimes when we don't give our weaker traits some nurturing focus, life steps in and forces us to pay attention. We can start the process of personal growth by taking responsibility for ourselves in what we say, how we say it, what we do, and how we treat ourselves and others. We need to be willing to let go of those old habits, such as stubbornness and needing to be right, and embrace learning new ways of thinking and relating to others. We can learn how to stop and think before we react and learn how to take our time to reflect and respond appropriately. We need to learn how to treat ourselves with more respect by letting go of our old, disparaging self-appraisals and negative self-beliefs. We can also learn how to stop being judgmental and be more accepting of the different beliefs various people hold. Further, we can develop the empathy needed to truly understand others when they are suffering hardship and know when to offer our support.

These are just some thoughts that can help us on our self-development journey. Whatever it is that we need to develop in ourselves, it comes down to committing to our personal growth and being aware of the areas in our lives that require attention for further development. This always starts with self-acceptance, being able to appreciate and fully accept who we are at any given moment, and being mindful of the areas in which we want to grow and become the best versions of ourselves. Embracing new ways of thinking and being is a brave move, as we will encounter challenging experiences when we engage in changing those things we want to change. Thus, we are daring to believe we can overcome obstacles in our lives that have caused us problems in the past. It's well worth the effort as those positive changes we initiate have the potential to take us to another dimension of ourselves and give greater meaning to our lives. This enhances our abilities to become even more empowered!

One final word on this matter. Remember to be especially kind to yourself when you're making changes and going through personal growth as it will come with challenges. Recognising and confronting our shortcomings can be incredibly difficult, and then making the changes adds another layer. Change and personal growth are not for the faint-hearted but for the brave hearts out there! Remember we are not perfect; nor will we ever be. We will continue to learn lessons throughout life, which will often occur due to consequences to the choices we make. And that will always be how it is in this world. When we make mistakes, it's important to refrain from beating ourselves up but rather to engage in self-acceptance, taking on board the lessons we learn as we move forward. We can even congratulate ourselves if we see we've overcome an old habit and recognised the change has resulted in rewarding outcomes.

Optional Exercises

These following suggestions may help you to explore any areas of your personal life you feel could contribute to your personal growth. There may be other areas not mentioned here that you can identify that need attention. Please approach this by giving attention to your personal needs, and remember to remain kind to yourself.

Things to Ponder

- Do I have a tendency to always want to be right?
- How does the need to be right affect all my relationships?
- What areas am I aware of that need personal growth?
- Am I open to listening to other people's points of view?

- Do I progressively learn by my own experiences and what I see in others?
- How stubborn am I, and does this serve me well?
- Where do I think I am on the empathy scale from 0 to 10?

Things I Can Do

- Challenge my own need to be right by considering the opinions of others.
- Practice empathy by also looking at situations from the other person's perspective.
- Make a plan to practice positive self-reflection.
- Set certain goals towards making positive changes.
- Practice being true to myself whilst avoiding the tendency to engage in stubborn behaviour.
- Write in my journal what I'm learning about myself.

CHAPTER SEVEN

EMBRACING YOUR UNIQUENESS

There is only one you, so do your best to make it count!

This topic takes us to another level in our relationship with ourselves and allows us to explore who we are with a deeper understanding. I believe the ability to embrace your character is an extension of your sense of self and is more about being able to express yourself and what you have to offer the world unashamedly and wholeheartedly. The reason this area is relevant to our relationship journey is because as we grow throughout our lives, it's important to understand ourselves enough so we can optimise our potential for success in our social world. When we get into a relationship, we need to know what things we can compromise on and those that are not negotiable. The ability for each of us to maintain our true character must be not negotiable. It is not something we can compromise on, so it's important to get this in place prior to navigating into the world of relationships.

It may be surprising that many have presented to therapy sessions over the years with a distorted or non-existent understanding of their own personality. Some have spent their whole lives with poor self-esteem, unable to know or understand, let alone experience, their true character. Some have spent decades in a space of self-disparaging thoughts and beliefs about themselves. They sometimes present with a sense of shame about who they are, consumed with depression and anxiety, and lacking in understanding of the longstanding neglect toward personal expression of their true personality. There is a certain relief they experience when they eventually come to realise their own personality has some great qualities that are worthy of expressing openly.

After seeing how much negative self-belief clings on throughout life, I always encourage younger people to explore their understanding of who they really are, become acquainted with their true character, and learn how to express themselves. It makes a huge difference and will affect the decisions they make for themselves throughout their lives. It's also helpful to understand that we're each on our own journey and will grow and change over time, so we can also expect our character to develop further. We're not expected to have it all together when we're young, or anytime really. Therefore, allowing our character to grow is part of the process in our life journey. For this reason, we can remain true to ourselves wherever we are at any given time throughout our life journey.

Embracing one's character starts with total self-acceptance, as we've addressed in previous chapters. It's about daring to believe we're okay and addressing anything to the contrary. If we've held on to a negative view about ourselves, believing we are deficient and abnormally flawed, then we're being unfair to ourselves and need to make some adjustments. This is so easy to overlook when we lack knowledge and understanding and neglect to nurture our true character.

Overcoming this requires that we each dive deeper into our individual personality and embrace those things that make us unique and different from everyone else. We may find similarities with others just as we see differences, but there is only one you. I find it absolutely fascinating that out of all the billions of people in the world, each and every one of us is totally unique. That uniqueness is what's important to embrace, so we can fully experience being who we're meant to be in this world, leading us to find our purposes and values in life.

The obstacles that get in the way of embracing our true character has to do with the limiting beliefs about who we are, not knowing what we're capable of, and not understanding the power of our own minds. Many have been caught up in self-defeating states of mind, holding on to an underlying belief that they're not capable of doing the things they want to do, unable to change, and not being good enough in whatever the situation demands. This could not be further from the truth! If we continue to feed our minds with such negativity, we'll convince ourselves of our inadequacies and struggle to find solutions.

This raises the question, "Why is it that so many of us struggle with this issue?" As we've been learning, the answer always goes back to our earlier experiences. Somewhere, at some time, our experiences have convinced us that we cannot be successful in life. In fact, some people remain in a constant state of expecting to fail. This is not because they are failures, but failing is all they have known. That sense of failure is familiar to them, and it's what attracts their focus. Some families have had incredible hardships, leaving family members discouraged by things going wrong and struggling to believe it can be any different. We are strongly influenced by our childhood experiences, whether in the family environment or our school lives. We will generally continue with similar thought habits and beliefs that we became familiar with in our growing-up years. What we sometimes don't consider or understand is that we don't need to be stuck in that same pattern. Many have overcome this limiting self-belief system and turned their lives around, and you can too.

Perhaps I can provide an example of my experience through the recovery process from my earlier years. Like many others, I spent most of my young-adult life believing I was not good enough. When I confronted this and explored it further, I gained some insights, realising at the core of my being was an underlying belief that I was "broken." I came to understand that this belief had formed a veil through which all my life experiences were filtered. Everything in my life was affected by that sense that I was seriously flawed beyond recovery. That was how I internalised my understanding of myself. I could override it sometimes with an internal defiance, as I was rebellious, stubborn, and determined to fight for what I wanted to do in life. But the brokenness I felt was a constant undercurrent. For many years it influenced how I thought about myself, how I viewed my achievements, and the choices I made in my life. I made many mistakes, but I learned from them and eventually came to understand that it wasn't because I was flawed or broken. I learned that good and bad things happen to everyone, and while in our goodness, we can still make mistakes. I learned that this was just how things are in real life!

Character is a mighty force that we all have, and with that, the ability to overcome adverse life situations in spite of any hardships we have endured in our earlier lives. There is ample evidence of this in numerous stories that have been told throughout time all over the world. We are aware of all those rags-to-riches stories, especially the ones where people have come out of childhood hardship and made something great of their lives having reached outstanding achievements. It's a great reminder that it's not the adversities in life that determine well-being and happiness but how we handle them and what we do with them that really make the difference.

I don't say this lightly. I know that some have experienced dreadfully adverse situations during and sometimes throughout their entire childhoods that have damaged them significantly. For such people, much can be gained by seeking the right kind of therapy for whatever's needed to support and guide them through their healing process. What happened to us as children is not our fault. We have no reason to feel ashamed or carry that shame into adulthood. The problem with this whole deal is that when we become adults, we tend to look back at our child selves and judge ourselves as though we were adults. We don't seem to realise that children don't have the capacity to think, reason, and problem-solve as adults. If bad things happened to us when we were children, we weren't developed enough cognitively, psychologically, or emotionally to know how to deal with the situation. This resulted in bad feelings staying with us and eventually caused us grief, shame, and guilt that never belonged to us. Through this process, we can end up grappling with a lifelong pattern of self-defeating behaviours. But thankfully, as you'll be aware by now, it doesn't have to stay that way.

If we want to recover, it's necessary that we each grasp hold of the fact and understand that our mind has enormous power, and the way we think about ourselves will ultimately determine who we become. This will affect certain outcomes in our lives, so we need to stay vigilant about what we feed our minds. When we hold on to limiting self-beliefs by engaging in negative self-talk and poor opinions of ourselves, we damage ourselves. Some common self-defeating things people say to themselves are, "I'm such a loser," or, "I'm probably wrong. I usually am," or, "I don't have much to offer in life." Well, really, is that true? Or is that the way you have learned to think of yourself and have formed that belief habit? You weren't born with negative, self-defeating beliefs. You have learned them, so you can change them! If you feel trapped or stuck in your life situation, maybe it's time to change things, so you can develop your true potential and be the person who expresses the real you.

If you're relating to this, then perhaps it's time to reflect and get in touch with your true inner self. Do you have a healthy self-concept, or do you find you're constantly feeling bad about yourself? If the latter, then maybe this is an opportune time to make a healthy decision to make the change. Journalling can be helpful in processing such issues as you can do this in private, giving you the opportunity to explore where your self-defeating thoughts come from and prompting you to know what changes you want to make. You may prefer to seek therapy to help you sort it out. Whichever way you choose to address this, you will have the opportunity to make the positive changes you need to embrace your true character. As there is only one you, imagine what you may find out about yourself and your life purpose. You are not an extension of your parents; nor do you have to stay in the script of what life dealt you. You can decide that for yourself. You are uniquely you!

I have purposely addressed some of the difficult life situations that people have endured to provide an understanding that no matter what has happened to us, we can still overcome our limiting self-beliefs and learn how to find and express the best of ourselves. The same principle applies to everyone, whether we've had a wonderful childhood with no real dramas or we've suffered adversities. This is an empowering experience that we can all embrace. We can let go of self-defeating beliefs that have arrested personal growth and allow our true selves to emerge. There's no advantage to self-doubt, so let it go. Allow your true self to emerge, so you can be the person you were meant to be. Find your uniqueness and stay in it. You are enough, so search for your true purpose and step into it!

Optional Exercises

These exercises will help you to dig deeper into your sense of self by recognising any negative self-beliefs you may have and find ways to replace them with healthy ones. They may be challenging for some. If needed, you may benefit from seeking an experienced therapist who does Schema Therapy, IFS (Internal Family Systems) Therapy or another therapy that addresses your internal belief system.

Things to Ponder

- What is my true character?
- Do I allow my character to be seen by others?
- Do I have a negative self-view?

- What do I truly believe about myself?
- Have my early experiences held me back in my life?
- What do I need to let go of?
- What do I need to bring more of into my life?

Things I Can Do

- Monitor the way I think of myself and obstacles that stop me from embracing who I am.
- Address any obstacles that stop me from allowing my true character to be seen.
- Explore my uniqueness and what hidden talents I may have.
- Seek therapy if I have deep-seated issues that I can't move on my own.
- Make a commitment to start practicing being my true self, starting now.
- Embrace my true character; express myself, and be happy with who I am.

CHAPTER 8

YOUR SPIRITUAL SELF

Your spiritual self will inspire and guide you on your life journey!

Have you ever noticed specific times when you've had a deep inner knowing about something? You may have heard this referred to as being your "gut" instinct. This is probably the best and most realistic primary indication of having a spiritual awareness about something you're contending with at the time. It could be when making an important decision about something, about cautioning you against taking a step that you're not comfortable about, or about your involvement with people who come into your life. You may also notice that your head says something different to your heart and neither really match with what your gut instinct is telling you. I've noticed some people are more aware of this than others, though it is certainly a human function that's available to everyone. I believe when we take more notice of this, we become more attuned to it. And subsequently, we will gain some insight regarding what we need to do in any given situation.

Your spiritual self is an important part of who you are. And that is not about being religious but about having that deeper dimension to yourself—beyond the physical realm. This area is often neglected when considering our perception of our whole selves. There are many parts to "the self" we can identify with and name, such as our physical bodies, our emotional world, our thoughts and beliefs that make up our cognitions, our psychological selves, our social ways of being, and our spiritual selves. In this chapter, we focus on our spirituality as an integral part of our whole make-up that also requires our attention in order to express our wholeness. I believe our spirituality is connected to our sense of well-being and can make a significant difference in our lives—especially when making decisions.

I believe the spiritual self has intrinsic value to each and every one of us as it is the only part that instils hope—or promise—of living a better life, especially when we are experiencing challenges and hardships. When we're going about our daily business, we often don't have that on our radar. Our focus is more on what we can gain, how we can make more money, how to get more out of life, or just the everyday activities that consume our lives. When it comes to our spiritual selves, we tend to think beyond what is actually happening at the time and lift our horizons to contemplate the changes we desire for our lives. This will often become more evident to us during meditation or prayer times, depending on our belief system. I sometimes liken this experience to electricity being turned on. While we accept darkness because it's night-time, if we turn on the light, we can see what's around us. But if we don't turn it on, we stay in darkness. Embracing our spirituality is just like turning the light on as we will start to see things we didn't see beforehand.

I can speak with confidence about this because I have had spiritual experiences at different times in my life that left no doubt in my mind. They proved to me that we are part of a bigger picture that resembles a supernatural and spiritual world. What we see with our human eyes in our physical world is not all there is to this life. There's another dimension we can tap into by activating our belief systems, otherwise known as our faith. We're not just living our lives here on earth and then no longer exist. On the contrary. We existed before our human bodies existed, and we will continue on after our lives on earth are done. This is because each and every one of us has a soul, which is a small part of the essence of a Higher Power that lives within us and cannot be destroyed. It is absolutely indestructible!

I've known people to say they want proof of a spiritual world, and if there is no scientific evidence by traditional standards, they won't accept it. Some people choose not to believe in any Higher Power, no matter how it's presented. The interesting thing about this is that I am convinced everyone knows there is a Higher Power at some level in their being. The problem with wanting proof first is that faith is the conviction, the intrinsic knowing of what is not seen. Faith has to come before proof, not the other way around. If we have faith in someone's ability, but that person hasn't proven himself or herself yet, we believe the individual will produce what is expected. We can apply this principle to ourselves too, especially when we need to make changes in our lives that aim for the best of ourselves and the most favourable outcome for the common good. This is why we are sometimes encouraged to have faith in ourselves.

We have all experienced times when we've needed to have faith in ourselves. However, we also have an opportunity to have faith in a Higher Power. Whether we call that God, the Universe, Love or just our Higher Power, there is an energy that extends beyond our physical selves that is available to assist us through life. Some will refer to this as the Higher Self. In my understanding, this energy is available to everyone who seeks it. I make a point never to argue or debate with people about this. After all, everyone can believe whatever they choose. However, I have always known this part of life exists, and it has been a central part of my life for as long as I can remember.

I totally believe in science, so I can understand how difficult it is for the scientifically minded to understand faith. But I believe there is also evidence through other means gathered over time through people's experiences, more in line with qualitative research. Through recent studies in the field of quantum physics, there is evidence that our lives are merged into an energy field—the quantum field— that provides evidence of a supernatural space we are yet to fully understand. There are a multitude of books and other forms of literature presenting stories of individual experiences that provide evidence of the reality of our spiritual existence. Many accomplished, educated and scientifically minded people around the world testify to having spiritual awareness.

When we think about our lives and how we go through the many life challenges we're presented with, it makes no sense if it's all for nothing and that we no longer exist in any form. Seriously, what would be the point? Why would we go through all the difficulties and challenges in our lives if they weren't there to develop us in some way, teach us what we need to learn and bring more meaning into our lives? When we look back and think of the biggest challenges in our lives, can we see what they were about? What did we learn from them? How have we done things differently since? I believe we are continuously learning life lessons. And sometimes we learn them, and other times we don't.

Do you have any embarrassing experiences in your life that you just cringe about when they come to mind? I know I do! What about the mistakes we know we've made? We've all made them, however tiny or huge. When we learn by our mistakes, we generally change the way we do things, so we don't repeat them. If we don't learn from them, they seem to come around again, sometimes in different ways but with the same principles at play. When we are in touch with our spirituality, we are in a more humble and teachable position. Our egos don't have much of a say when we are authentically engaged with our spiritual selves. Ego and pride are not involved in matters of a spiritual nature. However, authentic humility and spirituality go hand in hand.

My spirituality has been an important part of my life since childhood. I had some profound experiences that got me through troubled times growing up in a dysfunctional, alcoholic family. Following from that, I learned that it made a big difference when I called on my Higher Power for guidance. The answers were always identifiable through my gut instincts, and I also learned what happened when I didn't take notice. This is why I'm addressing this topic. Being in touch with our spiritual selves can guide us into making good decisions in our lives. When it comes to choosing life partners, we can call on our Higher Power to guide and help us attract the right kind of person into our lives. Interestingly, we often see this only in hindsight, as things can happen in our lives that seem impossible or highly improbable.

My own story is a good example of this. My partner and I lived on opposite sides of Australia when we met. We were introduced by a mutual friend, who was insistent that we meet each other. She knew us both reasonably well. She spoke to each of us about the other and consistently encouraged us to connect, even if just to have a chat. She made comments to both of us how she saw us as being very similar and mentioned how we spoke of similar things in the same manner. I was absolutely opposed to this whole idea and definitely didn't want to become involved with someone who lived on the other side of Australia. I had family commitments that meant I needed to stay in Perth. Nevertheless, we eventually started to connect by email and phone over several months.

Well, this evolved over time. And after twenty-three years together, we are happily married with a wonderful extended family, including fabulous kids and step-kids with their partners, and a bunch of grandchildren that we share. For me, this came about by not trusting myself so much—due to my less-than-desirable relationship track record—but by trusting my Higher Power. Somehow, everything unfolded and worked out well. And this is another story, but for now, I just want to encourage you to be open to your spiritual self and learn how to trust your own Higher Power that is there to help meet your needs and give you the desires of your heart. At times your gut instinct will let you know when you need to move towards something or stay away from it. This is exactly what is necessary when we are in need of such vitally important guidance.

As we move into the next section, I trust you will have spent substantial and valuable time exploring your relationship with yourself—in all its facets—and are bursting with self-compassion and self-acceptance. If so, you'll be in a great place to be enjoying your life and getting on with doing the things you love to do. I also hope you are open to exploring your relationship with your spiritual self to make your path clearer. This will help you prepare for a successful next step. I hope you have absorbed all the questions and challenges necessary for the unique you because it's going to make all the difference to your success in your relationship journey!

PART 2
CULTIVATING GOOD RELATIONSHIPS

When you Know yourself – Can Be yourself – and Love yourself

Authentically...

You have laid the foundation needed to make better choices.

Choosing your partner wisely...

Creates the opportunity to give you a better life!

—Wendy J. Britten

CHAPTER 9

IDENTIFYING RELATIONSHIP PATTERNS

When the light comes on, the darkness disappears!

I must have had hundreds of people over the years who have come to see me in distress following a relationship breakdown and end up saying something like, "I don't know … I just seem to choose the same type of person every time!" This is often followed by, "They seem very different in the beginning. But somehow, the same issue emerges, and the relationship goes downhill very quickly." This is often followed with, "How did I not see that coming?" This seems to be more evident in women, but also some men, and anywhere from their late twenties through to their thirties or forties. Some even older. It generally follows a succession of failed relationships that have identifiable themes and a negative effect on people, sometimes causing them to feel like giving up altogether.

This problem can emerge with people at any age if they haven't already given up on relationships altogether. They often present with stories about a long line of horrendous relationships that, when explored, have a definite recognisable pattern. Some of the comments I've heard people say are, "That's it. No more relationships for me. I'm done!" I've even heard people say they've been told they shouldn't have more relationships because of their past failures. Of course, this is unfair and most definitely untrue. Everyone is capable of finding a suitable relationship, even if they think it's impossible. I notice when people say such things, especially younger individuals, they're deeply saddened by the prospect. I recognise that because I've been there, and I know how easily we can feel unwanted, unlovable, and desperately lonely all at the same time. If this is you and you have skipped the first part of this book, please go back and read it from the start!

The best time to work on getting this issue sorted is when you don't have a partner or if you're in an unhappy relationship and wondering whether to stay or leave. It took me several years of heartache to sort this one out, which is why I want to help others identify and break their own dysfunctional relationship patterns. Some will have already sorted this out without knowing exactly what's happened, and this is a delight to see. It does happen!

However, if you've grown up in a dysfunctional family, you're at greater risk of attracting the wrong kind of partner and more likely to be one of those who end up saying, "I've done it again! What am I doing wrong?" My heart goes out to them as I understand their anguish. They are not alone as many of us have travelled that road.

When I was working on my own pattern of failed relationships, I became consumed with self-help books. I'm forever grateful to those who wrote them, including Melody Beattie and Robin Norwood, as their books opened my eyes to so much. I'd been unaware of the patterns in my relationships, yet was able to relate to the different scenarios presented by the authors. I learned how to reflect on my own life and the conditioning I'd become accustomed to mainly because of how I saw myself in the world. I was studying at the time and sorted things out between talking to my peers and colleagues, reading my books, and learning about the many aspects of individual, couple, and family issues that cause disturbances in life. Together, and guided by my faith, this formed a significant part of my healing journey.

Throughout the earlier parts of those years after my second marriage failed, I was filled with intense pain and suffering. I was constantly fraught with guilt and shame simply for being me and existing. I had the deep sense that I didn't belong anywhere and had carried an "imposter syndrome" just for my existence in the world. I was desperate to find answers. I devoured those books, finding myself reading the same words over at times, and then interpreting my life as I compared what I was reading with what I was going through. My books became my constant night companions and my personal guides.

I became intrigued with relationships as my access to real cases and my learning capacity increased throughout my postgraduate studies. I started talking to others and soon became strongly aware of different relationship experiences. I found myself questioning specific circumstances in relationships and exploring contributing factors. And when exploring case studies, I started to take more notice of the family dynamics in people's families of origin. I began noticing specific patterns that emerged from people's families of origin into their relationship choices. What I found is that while unique patterns specific to individuals became evident, there were three patterns that emerged more frequently.

This has been validated by more than twenty years of private practice. I will use the following three scenarios to explain them. The names and stories do not apply to any particular person but are symbolic examples of real-life situations.

Jodie

Jodie was the second-oldest child in her family and she had three siblings. In the early years of her life, she was a daddy's girl. She adored her father, bonded with him early and stayed connected to him throughout her earlier childhood. Her older sister was very close to their mother, being similar in temperament, while Jodie was more outgoing, having a similar personality to her father. He was a policeman and quite strict, yet Jodie adored him. However, by the time she was ten years old, her father had left the police force, developed a serious drinking problem, and had become a full-on alcoholic.

For the next several years, the family experienced many intensely difficult times. The family's assets and finances were gradually depleted to the point that the family home was sold to pay accumulated debts. This resulted in the marriage breaking up, and the father being separated from the rest of the family who were left in severe poverty. Jodie was very angry with her father and ceased speaking to him. She concealed a very deep hurt and couldn't forgive him for destroying their family. This continued for many years.

Jodie was put in the position of being the extra parent after her older sister moved away from home. At sixteen years old, it was a role she wasn't equipped to take on. She struggled through her teenage years and married her boyfriend of three years at eighteen years of age. However, this did not end her sense of responsibility, which was very real and expected. Thus, she continued to look out for her mother and younger siblings after marrying. On later reflection, Jodie came to realise that she was desperate to marry so she could make a family of her own.

By the time she'd been married a few years, she realised her husband had a serious gambling problem that was fast getting out of control. Money started to disappear, and secret loans started to emerge. When Jodie became aware of the extent of his gambling, she left the marriage, which had only lasted six years.

A year later, Jodie began a serious relationship with a man who was a real charmer. She thought he was different from any other man she'd ever known and was drawn to his charismatic personality. They married eighteen months after her first marriage ended. Things started off okay, but several years into the marriage, she realised he'd been having multiple affairs. His womanising habits were so prolific they were off the charts. She eventually realised he had a serious sex addiction problem. She forgave him on numerous occasions after he promised he wouldn't do it again and begged her forgiveness. This became a cyclic pattern that lasted about sixteen years. During that time, Jodie forgave, supported, and tried to help him recover. He never did, so she eventually divorced him.

Jodie was oblivious to her own part in the men she had connected with, but when the therapeutic process allowed her to explore it further, she came to understand she was attracted to men who had addictions. She'd seen her partners as being very different but then recognised the pattern. When she examined all her attractions, including her short-term relationships, she was able to identify addiction as a common theme. She'd tried to heal the emotional wounds in her life by filling the gaps with what felt familiar, which was that addictive personality. She was then able to work on herself, gain an understanding of her true authentic self, built her self-esteem, and eventually came to understand what she really needed and wanted in a relationship.

Chloe

Chloe was an only child. She was raised by her mother with the support of her aunt and mother's sister, whose partner worked away in the mines. She never knew her father and was told that he disappeared after hearing her mother was pregnant. There were no secrets about this, and her mother was always honest and upfront with the real story.

Chloe had a reasonably happy childhood. But deep down, she longed to know her father. She would fantasise about meeting him, which she could do well as she had a great imagination. When she reached her teen years, she questioned her mother continuously, asking for details about her father, so she could try and connect with him. Through a chain of enquiries, she eventually found him, but he had married and had three other children with his wife. Sadly, he told her he couldn't tell his family about her and that she had to stay away.

Chloe was devastated, though had been well-aware of the possibility of this outcome. She sought therapy to work through this and was eventually able to put it behind her and move on with her life. By the time she was eighteen years old, she'd had a few boyfriends, but the relationships didn't last long. Then she met a boy a year older than her who was popular and had a large group of friends. This was different than Chloe, who was quieter in nature and only had a small group of girlfriends. She was strongly attracted to him; she believed she was in love with him. Chloe saw her boyfriend on the weekends as she was studying, and he spent time with his mates through the week. Several months into the relationship, he started making plans on the weekends with his mates and began cancelling arrangements he'd made with Chloe. This became increasingly hurtful to Chloe. It eventually became intolerable, so she ended the relationship.

She had several boyfriends following this. The first was undecided about whether or not he would go back to his former girlfriend, another who worked away five weeks out of six, and another who she later found out had been stringing her along and was already in a committed relationship. They all seemed painfully hopeless.

She then met someone at the same university she attended and formed a relationship that became longer-term. Chloe initially saw her new boyfriend as totally different from anyone she'd seen previously, and she had begun to feel hopeful about this relationship. Her boyfriend studied engineering, and things seemed promising for the first few years. They started to make marriage plans and decisions about where they wanted to live and what type of house they wanted. It all looked like it was turning into a dream relationship.

After they had been married for a few years, Chloe started to realise that something was missing. The relationship was built on practicalities, and there was no emotional connection. While he was a good man, she eventually realised he was unable to give her what she needed in the relationship. She craved for that deeper connection that never eventuated.

Chloe ended her marriage and subsequently started therapy. She had already started to recognise the pattern in her relationships and through therapy, was able to explore it further. Once she mapped out her relationship journey, she discovered that all along, she'd been attracted to guys who were unavailable. They seemed to be available in some ways, though when she looked deeper into the relationships, she could see there was a lack of emotional connection with all of them. This pattern started with her father, who was unavailable in every way. And when she contacted him, he was emotionally dismissive and continued to be unavailable. Chloe then had the opportunity to get to know herself better and consider her relationship needs before getting into another relationship.

Kalinda

Kalinda was raised in a chaotic family home of mother, father, and five siblings. She was the third child, with two older brothers and three younger sisters. Fighting was a regular occurrence in her home. She recalled being woken in the middle of the night as her parents yelled at each other, things were broken, and walls were thumped. Her father was a violent man with a terrible temper, and he never listened to anyone else's point of view. His word ruled the household, or the others would be on the receiving end of his wrath. Having two older brothers, Kalinda was not in the habit of being too soft and girly, so she would stand up for herself. She was resilient out of necessity to survive in her family.

Kalinda started dating at fifteen years old. She recalled only feeling comfortable with other kids who were rebellious and mostly came from troubled homes. She had several relationships throughout her teens that lasted between one and six months. She ended most of them due to being hit, punched, and verbally abused a few times too often.

Kalinda then met her next partner, who she stayed with for ten years. The relationship had been turbulent, though things would settle down and continue on until another issue heated up, and this would flare up another fight. Kalinda started to realise she was getting older and decided she didn't want to live the rest of her life like that. She wanted to have children and had flashbacks of what it was like growing up in her family. She couldn't bear the thought, so she ended the relationship.

She then met a white-collar worker who was so different from any of her previous partners. She couldn't believe he was interested in her and immediately fell madly in love with him. Things were great at the start. They seemed compatible in many ways; both enjoyed the outdoors and doing adventurous things together. They had dinner parties with couple friends on weekend nights, enjoying good company, food, and wine. Kalinda noticed her partner drank a lot more than anyone else at the dinners and started suggesting he take more notice of his alcohol intake. This didn't go well, and over time, he became angry with her to the point he started raising his hand to hit her, but she never thought he would. Then when they came home one night and she told him how disappointed she was in his behaviour, he struck her so hard across the face that she fell to the floor. She laid there in shock, unable to move for some time.

After he left the room in his drunken stupor and flaked out on their bed, she went to the spare room, where she could feel safer and try to get some sleep. Her tears mixed with the blood on her face. In the morning, she was acutely aware of her situation and knew she couldn't stay in the house with him any longer. Kalinda wasn't going to risk history repeating itself, and she could not believe she had landed herself in this position yet again! At thirty-eight years old, she felt desperate, alone, and convinced she would have to stay single because of her failed attempts at relationships. She figured it must be something about her and was certain she could never trust herself again.

Kalinda sought therapy and started examining the pattern in her relationships throughout her life. She was soon able to identify her blind spots. She was attracted to men who had an underlying tendency towards violence. Although she had some awareness of the similarities in her previous relationships, she hadn't picked up on the subtle signs in her more recent partner as it was well concealed. She later found out he had a history of domestic violence in his family of origin, which he had never mentioned. Kalinda had the opportunity to address her pattern of being attracted to violence-prone men. She was then able to develop her sense of self and learn how to be more discerning, allowing her to make better choices.

These scenarios depict the most common themes identified in those who find themselves in dysfunctional relationships; there are many more. In fact, some themes arose that I'd never heard before. They truly can be anything at all, and are often somewhat unpredictable. Some of the other more common patterns are attractions to those who are self-absorbed, narcissistic, compulsive liars, have weak personalities, are unethical, lawbreakers, poor communicators, or attention seekers. The pattern can be more common or completely unique, but either way, putting the work into identifying this is well worth the time and effort.

After identifying their own personal patterns, many have reacted by saying, "Wow, why didn't I ever see that?" There's no looking back once you know as you cannot un-know what you now know. This is the epiphany that's sometimes needed. However, for those new to relationships, developing your self-awareness and exploring your unique experiences growing up in your families of origin will help you to avoid falling into similar traps.

Wherever you are in your journey, you can work out your relationship pattern by identifying the common themes in your relationships. If it seems a bit obscure, don't worry. If there's a history of failed relationships, I guarantee there will be a pattern. For this reason, you may need to be patient and persevere, but as you do, you will work it out eventually, and it will be so worthwhile. Once you've worked out your pattern, don't despair. Read on to work out how to unravel the following parts of the puzzle. You may have some aha moments along the way, and my wish for you is that you do!

Optional Exercises

The following suggested tasks are designed to help you work out your relationship patterns. Don't worry if it's not clear. Things will unfold as you work through the rest of the book. Remember, this is a journey!

Things to Ponder

- Am I aware of my relationship pattern?
- What do I know about the people I am attracted to, and what is common among them?
- Do I need to further explore my relationship pattern?
- How vulnerable am I when it comes to getting into bad relationships?

- Have things worked out okay for me in my relationships?
- Am I attracted to good things or harmful things in partners?
- Am I being honest with myself about my attractions?

Things I Can Do

- Explore my relationship history to fully understand my pattern.
- Write a thorough description of every partner in previous relationships.
- Take a pen or highlighter to mark any similarities between partners.
- Journal or talk over with a close friend similarities and differences of previous partners.
- Reflect on my relationship with my parents and/or other adults involved in my upbringing.
- Notice how my relationship pattern reflects my relationships with either or both parents.
- Write in my journal to help me further explore and understand my relationship patterns.

CHAPTER 10

YOU IN YOUR FAMILY OF ORIGIN

Childhood experiences significantly influence our adult relationships.

We all leave childhood and enter adulthood with many messages about who we are in the world. These messages accumulate and form belief systems that can work for us or against us in our adult lives. We take on different opinions about ourselves based on how we've interpreted the words and actions of those in our environments throughout childhood. We've touched on some aspects of this reality in earlier parts of this book, especially when it's evident that entrenched negative belief systems are a result of childhood messages. We can now explore this more thoroughly and in the context of our relationships.

Those who were highly spirited as children may have been labelled as "naughty" or "bad" or the "rebel in the family." Others may have been tagged as being a bit on the "dumb" side if you can imagine that! Those who were quieter may have taken on the message that they are the "shy" ones or referred to in a way that made them feel ineffectual or unimportant. We can also take on positive messages from being referred to as bright, smart, academic, or savvy, tagging higher general intelligence. These messages—positive or negative—can impact us as we journey through our lives. If we've taken on the damaging labels others tagged us with, we need to challenge and reject them, so we can develop our own true sense of self and begin to heal from the damage from those earlier influences.

In family therapy sessions, people are often surprised about what their family members think of them. This is because we're not good at expressing ourselves well in families, and we don't always take on the messages that were intended. Rather, we can interpret them in more negative ways. This can be detrimental to how some people see themselves in the world as they've taken on impressions that were never intended. For example, someone who was constantly referred to as a "terror," the "rebellious" one, or the "dumb" one in their growing years could get the impression that there was something wrong with them, that they were the worst one in the family, and were not as important as their siblings. These are just a few of many negative self-beliefs that we may have taken on in our lives. Believe it or not, this is quite common and can have lasting adverse effects. Those affected can experience low self-worth. They can believe there's nothing they can do to change, so they accept the label for themselves and for how others see them.

Imagine a family of five people, a mother, father, and three children—a boy aged thirteen and two girls, fifteen and seventeen years old—attending a family therapy session. At some point during the session, the sixteen-year-old may say something like, "I know I'm not as smart as my brother and sister, so I'm not going to even try to do better at school. I'll never be as good as them so I gave up on that years ago."

Now, imagine a shock wave hitting the parents, maybe one more than the other. Imagine the look of horror on the parents' faces as they hear how their daughter sees herself in the family. This is a reality of the type of scenarios that come out in family therapy sessions. Family therapy is of great value as a therapeutic choice when addressing problems that arise in parenting or sibling issues. This is because it provides an opportunity for misunderstandings to be corrected, which will make a huge difference as to how that child sees herself or himself during future development.

In the above scenario, the word "smart" could be replaced with other words, such as, "attractive" or "good" or anything else she may have compared herself to, causing her to accept and believe a negative self-evaluation. The next part of the sentence would correspond to that word. For example, "I'm used to being ugly," or, "I'm used to being the bad one." Then there's that famous old saying, "I'm the black sheep in the family," which is often said in jest and sprouted as a common family joke. But it can unintentionally be harmful to the person concerned. Another comment often heard is, "I don't fit in this family," usually said by teenagers as they are growing older and becoming more self-aware.

If this belief becomes entrenched, it will leave the person with the sense of not belonging.

Birth order can also contribute to our sense of self and sometimes even impact how personality is shaped through childhood experiences. This can be whether you are the first born or the eldest daughter, growing up with a strong sense of responsibility from looking after your younger siblings, or you're the youngest child with less opportunities to developing your independence. This may cause difficulties in speaking up for yourself or lead to the need for more guidance and direction in making decisions. Alternatively, you could have been put on a pedestal and have an inflated sense of self-importance. You could be that middle child who just had to get on with things because you learned this way worked best. You may have become weary of too many rules that didn't make much sense to you, so you made up your own rules.

Whatever the situation, we are all in some way affected by our birth order. Of course, these themes are not set in stone as families are all unique and that, along with our individual personalities, will always have a huge impact on how we see ourselves in our social world once we leave the nest. For example, the oldest child is not always the most responsible, and the youngest child is sometimes the better decision maker. It all depends on the unique situations in families.

Our relationship with our parents also plays a major role in our self-belief. I often ask people when I'm getting to know them and exploring their family experiences, "Which parent do you identify with most?" Some will say both, but people will mostly align themselves with either their mother or father. This could be for a number of reasons, including their perception of intellectual ability, alikeness in personality, or for having chosen similar careers. Sometimes they'll identify with one parent about some things and the other parent about other things. For example, they may look more like one parent and see themselves as similar in personality to the other.

This identification forms part of that person's sense of self and can be a helpful way of exploring his or her self-worth and attraction to others in the world. Having a similar career to a parent can put pressure on someone if he or she feels the need to live up to that parent's expectations, such as doing things the same way or achieving the same goals. Being similar in personality can cause low self-esteem if that parent has let the family down in some way. Alternatively, it can encourage healthy self-esteem if that parent is well respected both inside and outside the family. These are just a few examples of many possibilities as we are affected by numerous contributing factors. However, the main point I want to make is that we're all influenced by the messages we get from our family of origin.

We are also influenced by our siblings and how we relate to each other, or whether we were an only child. Siblings often love to get under each other's skin, play-fight, or make fun of each other. While this is a normal part of child development in family situations, and children will mostly sail through with resilience on their sides, some of the messages can stick with people and influence how they see themselves later in life. If one sibling is favoured or seems favoured by a parent, the others can interpret this as though they are flawed as a person, which can cause them to think lowly of themselves throughout life. Likewise, school experiences that involve being bullied by others or being able to bully others influence a person's sense of self.

Those who've grown up an only child will sometimes struggle with their sense of self because they've not had other children in the family to measure themselves against. This may cause an overinflated sense of self or an insecure sense of self; both will impact how they make decisions and get along in the world. In some cases, they may have corrected this by having a healthy selection of friends or cousins who helped to bridge that gap and have avoided some of the pitfalls. In other situations, they have managed to develop a healthy sense of self due to good parenting and having a stable personality.

On another matter, twins can have their own set of struggles. This includes having to deal with being compared to a twin their entire lives by almost everyone they know, by being so closely connected with each other, and later, by striving for their ongoing needs for individuation. They will also be influenced by other factors that are unique to their particular situations, some of which will cause challenges and others that will create a healthy, positive self-belief system. Understanding these influencing factors may be helpful when issues arise later in life that affect the sense of self.

As you can see, we've all taken on beliefs about ourselves in the world that are based on a whole lot of messages we received while growing up. When it comes to seeing ourselves in relationships, we'll often be attracted to partners who help us maintain our self-beliefs, whether positive or negative. This happens mostly at a subconscious level, and we may or may not become aware of it in the process of our journey. This is why it's important to take an honest, authentic look at some of the experiences you've had during your childhood. You can then explore within yourself to identify the messages that have influenced your beliefs about yourself. For example, if you tend to be responsible for everyone else, how did that get to be there? If you feel insecure or needy, how did that come about? If you don't ever give yourself a voice, or if you don't like to listen to anyone else's opinions, how did those ideas become part of your mindset? And what impact does that have on your sense of self? Whatever the situation, you can explore it and learn a whole lot more about yourself in the process.

Thankfully, we all have the ability to address these issues and make the necessary changes in our personal belief systems, so we can see our needs as being different to what they otherwise would have been. If we believe we're inadequate, for example, we can prove to ourselves how untrue this is and then choose to take on a different self-belief. We will see that we have to be adequate because that is how we were born—absolutely good enough! If we engage in extreme or negative behaviours, while it may have served a purpose earlier in our lives, they are likely to be out of place in our adult world. It's to our advantage that we're brave enough to face those things that have given us false messages about ourselves and correct them. In contrast, we need to consider the good messages we've received throughout our lives as they can help us to validate all our experiences and affirm our strengths.

As we grow into adulthood, we develop the capacity to reflect on our personal belief system, which shapes how each of us will see ourselves as an adult. This will have a significant effect on the choices we make in our lives. It is why it's best to know ourselves first before getting into long-term relationships and why the first part of this book is dedicated to self-awareness. When we get into relationships, we each have the opportunity to explore further our sense of self as we get to know how we are as part of a couple. Developing a strong and secure sense of self individually makes that next layer of being with a partner more informative, paving the way to gain greater understanding about the quality of the relationship. We learn about ourselves in relationships that will shape our choices towards finding suitable partners. This is part of the process, and being aware of this may prevent some people from making learning relationships into permanent ones that don't survive the long haul.

When we are aware of our individual role in our family of origin, we gain a deeper understanding of ourselves, which impacts significantly the choices we make in choosing our relationships. We will be attracted to whatever seems comfortable to us, whether good or bad. If we believe we are not good enough, are unlovable, are over-responsible or too reliant on others, then we are likely to be attracted to those who will keep us in that state of belief. However, if we've done the work on ourselves and believe we are enough, that we are lovable, and have a good sense of our true responsibilities, then we're in a good position to make better choices regarding suitable, compatible partners.

Optional Exercises

The following considerations are about your perceived role in your family of origin and what you can learn about yourself. It may be helpful to identify other family members' roles to help you with the following questions and suggestions.

Things to Ponder

- What was my role in my family of origin?
- How has my birth order or situation affected me in my life?

- What messages have I taken from my family of origin?
- How do those messages affect how I am in my relationships?
- Do I have any negative labels that I need to challenge, reject, and change?
- Do I need to talk to someone about this and seek further help?

Things I Can Do

- Draw up a map of my family members (an opportunity to be creative).
- Identify the various roles that have been assigned to each family member.
- Journal my thoughts about my role in my family of origin and how I am affected.
- Explore and identify how my labels have affected me in my past relationships.
- Create a new ideal for what I want to believe in myself for my future.
- Consider what I want my role to be in my relationships moving forward.
- Set some goals for myself to reinvent my self-perception.

CHAPTER 11

BECOMING DISCERNING

Can I be my authentic self in this relationship?

What does it mean to become discerning, and why is it so important? If you've just read the previous chapters, you'll be starting to become aware of the difficulties we can encounter when trying to find that special person in our lives. It requires that we develop a wise understanding based on how well we know ourselves of who we choose to have in our lives. When it comes to our friends, we generally have those friendships because they are people we like to spend time with, and over time, we have developed a certain trust. When it comes to those we don't know yet, we're unsure in the beginning about whether we want to become more friendly with them. This is where discernment comes into the equation. Over time, we need to figure out whether this is a good connection. This is especially important and totally necessary when choosing partners. If we look at the definition of "discernment," we will find that it means having good judgement, being selective, refined, and cultivated in our thoughts and appraisals.

While we go through this process, it's important to remember to be respectful towards those we seek to know further. This is easier to do when we are more secure with ourselves as we're less threatened by differences and situations that could have otherwise been triggering. This is how we can maintain our authentic sense of self without losing ourselves in a relationship. We can stay aware, discerning what may or may not be good for us, so if necessary, we can know when to say, "It was nice to meet you. Goodbye."

As we know, authenticity refers to being true to ourselves and being who we are with full self-acceptance and positive self-regard. It means being honest with ourselves and being okay with who we are without thinking we need to be different. It definitely does not mean we need to alter ourselves to be how we think our partners want us to be. This is why one of the best ways of knowing if we are in a good relationship is to ask ourselves, "Can I be my authentic self in this relationship?" If we have to change things about ourselves to be in a relationship, we need to question what we're doing there. If you find yourself caught in this situation, you may need to recognise and address it, so you can put yourself back on track. If we cannot be ourselves because our partners require us to be different from who we are, then we may be in the wrong relationship. When this happens, something needs to change or the relationship may need to come to an end.

Too many people have gone through their lives getting caught up in being the person they thought their partner wanted, only to discover the whole relationship was a sham. Those relationships either break up or become entrenched in co-dependency, where one partner dominates, and the other submits at the cost of losing his or her true self. This is similar to the concept of becoming the "enabler," a term that's been used in alcoholism literature to describe someone who adapts himself or herself at length, enabling a partner to continue with the dysfunctional behaviour. But this doesn't only apply to alcoholics. It applies to any kind of self-serving or dysfunctional behaviour someone may be engaging in that causes the partner distress in the relationship. Sadly, those who engage in enabling behaviour generally do anything to keep the peace and protect themselves, even though the cost is losing themselves in the process.

I'm aware that this is a loaded topic and may be pressing buttons for some. It would certainly have pressed my buttons at earlier times of my life. If you're affected by this, you may want to seek professional advice, and talk your situation through with a psychologist skilled in dealing with relationships. This can give you peace of mind and provide a catalyst for making positive changes in your relationship. No relationship is perfect, just as no person is perfect. Therefore, when we come across new information regarding our relationships that shows up our blind spots, we have the opportunities to make positive changes. This is true whether or not we're already in an established relationship.

There are many situations in which relationships can be restored and don't necessarily have to end. Some couples are able to repair the injuries, restore their connections, and make the relationships so much better once they're aware of the areas that caused them problems. By engaging in therapy with a skilled relationship therapist, couples can prevent years of distress and anguish about their relationship when problems emerge. By understanding the dynamics in their relationship, couples can develop their awareness, improve their connections, and move into a more secure place. Alternatively, it may be an opportunity to end the relationship if there's a lack of cooperation and things are not going to work out.

From a personal perspective, in my recovering years, it became clear to me how much I had become accustomed to walking on eggshells. This is another comment I've heard many times from people in similar situations. That persistent need to stay in a relationship is based on an intense fear of failure, especially in subsequent marriages, and those affected would do almost anything to keep it together. I also wrongly thought I was doing the right thing by keeping my family intact. When I look back at those years and even though I now understand, I'm still horrified. There were times following my failed relationship when I actually gasped aloud as I recalled a memory. I would find myself saying, "How could he do that to me? How dare he do that! What kind of person could do that?" This would often be accompanied by a whole lot of angry outbursts towards both him and myself.

Once I got it all off my chest—like we sometimes need to do—this perspective morphed into, "Why did I let him do that to me? Why did I allow myself to be treated that way? What on earth was I thinking?"

My mother's voice was in my head by then, saying, "Nothing has the power to upset you unless you let it!" Hmmmm.

Then the big question to self: "Why did I stay there for so long? Seriously?" And then an exasperated, "Aagghh," (*me groaning in frustration*). It took quite a few similar episodes to get this under control. I'm happy that it's now long gone—a thing of the past, and I am so grateful for those life lessons learned and that I can help others travelling similar journeys.

At this point, I want to highlight an important observation regarding the difference in those previous two perspectives, about how I approached the situation and the things I said to myself. In the first perspective, I perceived myself as the victim, while in the second, I've demonstrated my need to take responsibility for my part in the relationship. I needed to own the fact that I enabled the process to continue. My mother was right! I was consumed with anger and wanted to blame my partner for the damage he caused, seeing him as the sole culprit in the situation. I've heard so many stories from people who had similar relationship experiences and wanted to blame and punish their former partners. This doesn't get them off the hook because obviously, if they were being abusive, they were responsible for the larger part of the problem.

However, the thing that makes a huge difference is the ability to take responsibility for what is within our power. The only thing we each have in our power is to take responsibility for our own part. We have no power over what another person does. In my situation, I allowed myself to be treated poorly by staying in the relationship. Then as I continued to stay, I allowed it to go on and did not give myself permission to bring it to an end. I was not fully aware at the time that I couldn't change him, and I never could. I realised that I had no power over what he did at all. I only had power over myself and what I chose to do. This was when I became empowered, when I discovered the power that belonged to me. Eventually, I did what I needed to do for myself and my family and got out!

Once I got out of the relationship and went through my initial healing and recovery process, I started to really experience what it meant to be empowered. It was a massive time of change for me and a time of reckoning. I came to realise that my life had never been without drama and stress for as long as I could remember, and it was time to confront myself regarding all the decisions I'd made and take control of my life. I had to address those times when I didn't listen to my gut instincts. I had to learn how to be myself and respect who I was as a person. At that time, I made a vow to myself that I would never allow anyone into my life who would treat me poorly again. I started to become aware of myself enough to know about my personal vulnerabilities and that I had the power to choose my path. This was the beginning of a new journey that would empower me towards a better life.

If I can do this, then anyone can! We can all take a stand and recognise the power we have in our lives and that we are responsible for how we allow ourselves to be treated. We can choose who we want to have in our lives, and we can just as easily decide who we don't want. We have the power to make all kinds of choices for ourselves, and we need to understand this along with the consequences of those choices we make. We have no power over what others do or say or over things in the past. But we do have power over what we choose to do, what we say, and who we allow in our lives. This is how exercising discernment plays into our ability to become empowered.

Empowerment and discernment go hand in hand as they both play a major role in our recovery after being in dysfunctional relationships. Both concepts will help guide us in our relationship choices. We need empowerment to be fully aware of our strengths and our abilities to do the best we can for our lives. And we need discernment to understand our patterns and to make good choices. In fact, empowerment comes from being discerning about the choices we make and from gaining the ability to make better decisions for our lives. When we remain true to who we are, being our authentic selves, and discern what is right or wrong for ourselves, empowerment comes into the picture and keeps us strong. We have the power to decide for ourselves regarding what we will do in any situation.

I am forever grateful for learning about how to become discerning in my life, especially in my choice of relationships. It helped me to develop my intuitive ability, to sharpen my instincts about what is right or wrong for me, and to be empowered enough to take necessary actions to improve my life. I'm still learning and always will be as we need to stay aware, so we don't slip back into our old familiar habits. However, my awareness radar keeps me on track, and I am most grateful to have survived the journey.

I sincerely hope you are inspired and find comfort in hearing about my personal experiences. Know that you can become empowered in whatever situation you are in by taking notice and being discerning about your life choices. Becoming discerning is possibly the most important thing we can do to cultivate good relationships.

The following Serenity Prayer is the Alcoholics Anonymous prayer, which I've known since childhood due to my mother's involvement with Al-Anon. Its wisdom entered psychological treatments in the past two decades, mostly associated with Acceptance and Commitment Therapy (ACT), and Mindfulness Therapy to encourage us towards acceptance of how things are and to focus on where our power lies.

God grant me the serenity to accept the things I cannot change …
Courage to change the things I can and
wisdom to know the difference.
(Reinhold Niebuhr)

This is discernment and empowerment in action!

Optional Exercises

The following suggestions are designed to help you identify areas of discernment, especially where you can see you have had blind spots, being unaware of some of the decisions you have made in the past. Stay honest with yourself as you consider the following.

Things to Ponder

- How discerning am I really?
- Is this something I need to give more attention to?
- What do my patterns tell me about my level of discernment?
- What sorts of people do I invite into my life?
- Do I allow people to treat me poorly in any way?
- Do I take responsibility for my part in the relationship?
- Do I feel empowered in the decisions I make?
- Am I allowing myself to be a victim by not stepping into my empowerment?

Things I Can Do

- Check my relationship pattern for signs of co-dependency.
- Journal my thoughts about my own pattern of accepting bad behaviour.

- Monitor how I speak about my story to see if I present myself as a victim.
- Take an inventory of how I can claim responsibility for my part in past relationships.
- Make a commitment to myself that I will be more discerning in the future.
- Practice self-empowerment by taking responsibility for my actions or non-actions.

CHAPTER 12

NO REGRETS AND THE SILVER LININGS

Be grateful for all the wonderful silver linings!

While writing this book, life threw a huge learning experience into the equation, as life does constantly. It continues to teach us deeper lessons through what's happening right in that moment of time. Just yesterday, I attended the funeral of my ex-mother-in-law, who passed away at the grand age of ninety-six. What an achievement of longevity. And what a life she had, dealing with all life's challenges and achievements just as everyone else does. I went with my eldest daughter, who was her biological granddaughter, and to me, it all felt so wonderful and produced such a rich experience as we both connected with family members who were a big part of our lives many years ago.

The love and acceptance among everyone became warmly exhilarating as we sought out old familiar connections. We reminisced over some great stories from the days when we were young and spent so much time together. The connection between my first family of in-laws and myself was undeniable, and I felt so comfortable reconnecting with them. We reminded each other of times almost forgotten and of all the fun and adventures we enjoyed together. But most of all, we remembered the bond we shared as extended family members who all got along so well. I'm sure many will relate to this kind of connection as we can form strong bonds with our partners' families that feel as strong as our own sometimes.

I guess the thing that struck me most was not something I didn't know already; it was more an infusion of a fuller extent to what I already knew. It wasn't the first time I'd seen the people in this family since leaving the relationship. We'd attended other family gatherings together and met up at other different times. I have also kept in touch with one of my sisters-in-law over the years. We went to school together and happened to marry two brothers of the same family, so we have known each other since teenagers. We also have things in common sharing similar beliefs and values, which has kept us connected over time.

The cause of my recent epiphany was the awareness of how much I had connected with this family back in the beginning and how much they meant to me. Although I already knew this, it was like a reawakening of the love and connection that I had with this family. As my own family had disintegrated as it did, I was desperate to find some joyful family time, and this family provided that for me at such a crucial time of my life. They all had such a shared, weird, dry sense of humour, and the bantering that went on was hugely infectious, something that I had been craving and joined in with wholeheartedly. Humour was something I had shared with my father as he was a very funny man when he wasn't drunk, and sometimes when he was! I was reminded that this connection had filled that space in me that was missing since my childhood.

I just loved the whole experience of reconnecting with these people, and they made it clear they were so happy to see me. It's always a wonderful feeling when you see people's eyes light up when they see you. The family is quite large; there were six siblings and a cousin with her husband who were also a big part of the clan. I had a great relationship with all of them. This was enough to remind me of what I had gained from this wonderful family. I found myself thinking; *Wouldn't it have been terrible if I'd never known them?* I have to acknowledge that this family gave me what I needed at the time to continue on with my life in a safe way and to later have the fortitude to leave it and find my own way in life.

Those memories led me to thinking about my next family of in-laws, who I also fell in love with hook, line, and sinker! They were a very spiritual family. In fact, both families were expressive of their faith in their own individual ways. The second relationship was a rocky road in the beginning for me because my second husband had been married previously, and his father was not going to accept anyone else to take the place of his son's first wife. He was obviously very close to and connected with her and could not understand why the relationship had ended.

The non-acceptance passed quickly, and I was welcomed into the family along with my two-year-old daughter, who they welcomed into their hearts almost immediately and wholeheartedly. She was pretty cute, so that wasn't a difficult thing to do. We soon became part of their clan, and although they lived in a different state, we got to see each other now and then and kept in touch on a regular basis. I inherited some great sisters-in-law with their husbands and children, and a fabulous step-son.

There's so much more I could say about this family, but the point of writing about this is that when I reflect, this was another incredible experience with wonderful people that I could not imagine being without in my life. Two whole families that I belonged to at different times who added so much richness to my life that could not be forgotten or discounted in any way. I was so blessed to have them all and have no regrets about my time with them. It was all part of my relationship journey on my life path. I remain forever connected to them both as I have a daughter from each marriage, and both families were fully accepting of them both. However, this did not all happen without casualties.

I understand how some of my poor choices and decisions affected my daughters. I've needed to come to terms with that, enduring the guilt and shame, and eventually allowing myself to heal. I spent many moments through the years berating myself for not leaving my second marriage sooner as it caused so much heartache and pain. My daughters suffered throughout their childhoods, which I would never intentionally allow to happen. This resulted in them having to deal with their own issues, both pursuing their individual healing journeys, and learning how to look after themselves and protect themselves emotionally. I am so proud of them as they are wonderful humans, excellent parents to their children, and are following their passions. I could not have asked for anything more. They also both managed to eventually find themselves in great relationships with amazing partners who give them the love and respect they deserve.

You may be able to relate to my story in some way if you have a history of failed relationships, or you may have an entirely different story but recognise how your choices affected outcomes in your life. No matter what has happened to you and your children, if you have them, you have the ability to make your life great. The reason I'm telling my story is so that you, too, will be able to reflect on your experiences and find your own silver linings. I've heard many stories about families following divorce and separation, and more often than not, there are strong connections between people and their former in-laws. Some of these connections play important roles in our self-development through certain periods of our lives and can positively influence our personal growth.

Finally, what I want to say about regrets is that we really have no need to have them at all! Many of us have been through troublesome times with a history of failed relationships in our wake. However, what's important is that we can move on with our lives and appreciate what we have. We can do this by letting go of the past, not allowing ourselves to engage in self-pity or, "Woe is me," parties that allow us to hold on to guilt and shame. Instead, we can make more positive choices about how we want to live in the future. We can get on with our lives, counting our blessings and being grateful for all our experiences, especially the ones that gave us our fabulous silver linings.

I truly believe that life is a gift, and it's our individual responsibility to live it to the fullest. There are so many wonderful things to be grateful for, and with this in mind we can let go of regrets, and stop wallowing in our miseries of the past. That will only hold us back in our ability to turn things around and make our lives great. If we want to continue being empowered in our lives, we can do so by deciding to let go of things beyond our control, cease blaming others for our woes, and move on with our lives from wherever we are right now. We can decide to be responsible for our own decisions and lives moving forward. The power is in our own hands for which direction we take. This is just another life choice!

Optional Exercises

The following considerations are to help you free yourself from past decisions that continue to haunt you. They are further designed to help you put the emphasis on your own silver linings and be incredibly grateful for them.

Things to Ponder

- Am I holding on to regrets?
- Do I blame myself for things that have not gone well?
- Do I blame others for everything and play the victim card?
- Do I act like a victim when I think or talk about my previous partner?
- What are some of the silver linings I can recognise in my failed relationships?
- What connections from previous relationships do I have that are special to me?
- What lessons have I learned from previous relationships and their families?

Things I Can Do

- Journal my thoughts and feelings about what I learnt in previous relationships.

- Consider and cherish the special connections I've made through previous relationships.
- Talk over with someone close about the silver linings I may have overlooked.
- Make a commitment to myself that I will let go of the past and focus on my life now.
- Seek professional help or someone to talk to if I am feeling bitter and unforgiving.
- Recognise my power in the decisions I make regarding future relationships.

CHAPTER 13

ATTRACTION

Insights into our attractions empower us to make better choices.

Let's take a close look at the topic of attraction, so you can explore your relationship history to see if you can identify some particular features that attract you in a potential partner. This is an interesting conversation to have with people, and I have come to know through my experiences in therapeutic situations that there are many features to which people are attracted. When I look back over my life and confront myself with what I've been attracted to, I can see that some of the smallest, seemingly insignificant details have influenced my attractions and sometimes impacted my choices in partners. This also bears a strong similarity to what I have heard from others.

When I ask people what attracted them to their partners, without a doubt, the most common answer is about looks! I have heard things like, "He was so good looking," "She was such a spunk," "It was his eyes," "He was a real hottie," "She had a fabulous body," "He reminds me somehow of my father when he was younger" (you could replace father with brother or sister or some other family member). You get the picture here. The attraction was either about something quite superficial or related to something that may have seemed meaningful but without much substance.

Such superficial attractions can give people all sorts of warm and fuzzy feelings that make them think they've fallen in love. The problem with this attraction is that it can be so misleading. And because it was a primary attraction, the other, more important things have not had such an influence on the love-struck romantic. To avoid this happening and being hoodwinked by the so-called love at first sight phenomenon, it's worth paying attention to our attractions and asking those what and why questions. We need to ask ourselves, "What is it that I am attracted to?" and, "Why am I attracted to this person?"

If physical attraction is the main thing that's drawn us to potential partners, there's a high risk of becoming established in a relationship that will later bring some surprises that are not so attractive. This means there's a good chance the relationship may not turn out to be what you really wanted. When the partner's real personality emerges, you may find that there are things about him or her you have difficulty accepting. And it could take you months or years to figure out what's gone wrong. By then, the relationship may be established, and it may be a whole lot more difficult to end. This becomes further complicated if we happen to start a family in that early stage as there is an extra layer to consider, making it even harder to leave the relationship. Many have stayed for the sake of the children.

Other common traits people discover about their partners a little later are things like having a bad temper, a nasty streak, a tendency to be violent, a destructive addiction, or being emotionally or physically unreachable, mean-spirited, controlling, tight or obsessed with money, uncommunicative, neglectful towards you, unable to stay faithful, overly entitled, or self-absorbed, to mention a few. I know many people reading this will be able to identify with some of these issues and recognise how they have been trapped at some point, causing them incredible suffering and disappointment. Some will have become aware sooner and been able to end the relationship earlier, enabling themselves to move on to something better.

Another common answer to the question is, "I don't know. There was just something about him [or her] that I was drawn to, and I really believed he [or she] was the one." In such circumstances, people could have been drawn to a range of features. And really, they could be anything, but nothing of real substance. This can be another danger signal for getting into a relationship for the wrong reasons, with no real evidence of what the person is really like. There's no way of really knowing whether this is someone he or she really wanted to be with, especially for the longer term. This is a very "pie in the sky' way of approaching a relationship, and needs a lot more than just the initial hunch. Sometimes the hunch could be right, but more often than not, it will be another way of leading us down the wrong track, and we waste time on someone who is never going to be right. Either way, it's well worth being aware and not allowing yourself to be caught up on a hunch alone.

The main difference in the hunch approach is that it depends on the person's early experiences. If we take the example of a young woman who's grown up in an environment that encouraged her belief in herself, she has a good chance of choosing well. This happens when she knows she is worthy and valuable. She's had loving role models in her parents and knows she matters. What she has to say counts, and people care about her opinions. She has been reassured that she is beautiful and loved. And above all, she has had a father or father figure who has looked out for her and made her feel worthwhile. This is the kind of experience that provides a good chance of having more trustworthy hunches.

In contrast, for a young woman who had the opposite of that nurturing upbringing and grown up not believing in herself, not really knowing how to look after or consider herself, doesn't really know who she is, and has no idea of her self-worth, the attraction is likely to be misleading. If you can relate to this, unless you have done a whole lot of work on your sense of self, beware of your hunches!

Don't despair, however, because you can change what you're

attracted to by building your self-esteem through working on your sense of self and creating some new boundaries and rules for your life. This is why it is so important to put the time and energy into developing your sense of self. If you neglect to do this, you become vulnerable to continue having the same challenges in future relationships.

It doesn't always work out this way though. I've known some of the most beautiful people who had the best of upbringings—with parents who are loving, kind, and gentle—with a generous and giving nature, and have attracted the complete opposite. I wonder sometimes if people have such great role models in their parents that they expect others to be the same and are sorely disappointed when they learn this is not the case. People in this situation are most likely unaware of self-absorbed people in the world who only consider themselves as worthy of attention and needing to have everything go their ways. Therefore, they can become vulnerable to being taken advantage of by potential partners. Self-absorbed people will seek out those who are the most giving of themselves.

There are so many possible explanations for people's attractions to each other, which is why it's important to observe and consider our own unique circumstances.

Another common reply to the attraction question is, "He [or she] seemed like a really nice person." Seeing that someone is a nice person on the first few meetings is not enough to enable us to make a call on the intention of that person or the quality of the connection. In fact, if someone appears too charming, beware of the possibility of narcissism lurking in the background. As one who has experienced this, I can say that it's not much fun down the track, when the underlying personality emerges. This is not always the case, thank goodness, and there are many people who are genuinely nice people who everyone likes. But a large part of a narcissistic personality is the "charm" factor. A narcissist will charm the pants off everyone they meet (sometimes literally) and have those people thinking he or she is the best person they ever met. This is only their charismatic charm shining through. It does not reflect the underlying disturbed personality.

After some time in the relationship—after a few dates, weeks, or months—the true attitude and behaviour begins to show through and will be noticeable. This is because they cannot keep up the facade for too long, and the pendulum will swing the other way as they demonstrate grandiose, self-absorbed, dismissive behaviour obsessed with their own self-importance. They also generally lack empathy. You may be left feeling bewildered and confused, not knowing what to make of it until you become more aware of what narcissism looks like. What most people do in the interim is to make excuses for their partners' bad behaviour, especially when they're rude and have upset others such as your family members and friends. These excuses sound something like, "Oh, he's just had a bad day," or, "Her brother just upset her." You get the drift.

Unfortunately, narcissism has become more prevalent in our world today, so it's important we become aware of its features when looking for a relationship. If you've ever met someone who was referred to as a "Jekyll and Hyde," you may have encountered a narcissist. If you start to see drastic changes in a new partner in a reasonably short period of time, going from "amazingly great," to "Whoa, what happened to Mr. Nice Guy [or that lovely girl]?" then do your own personal research to explore the person further and the reason for your attraction to him or her. You may save yourself years of pain and suffering. Books on narcissism have become readily available in recent years, so it is easier to explore if you are affected by narcissism.

Interestingly yet logically, it's also quite common to be attracted to someone who has similar characteristics to one's opposite-sex parent, and sometimes the same-sex parent. This may depend on which parent the person identifies with mostly. People who grow up with a parent who has serious problems, as mentioned previously, may be attracted to potential partners with similar personality or physical features.

There have been several explanations for this phenomenon. The main ones include the belief that people are recreating the relationship based on their earlier family experiences in an attempt to resolve the problems they encountered; they have some genetic predisposition; it's about history repeating itself because that's what happens; and it's about being drawn to a familiar dynamic that makes the person feel comfortable, thus creating a comfort zone.

This last explanation seems to make the most sense and is one that I generally see as being the most valid reason for being attracted to someone who is similar to a parent. When we meet potential partners, there's a certain sense that accompanies the connection that is often quite tangible from the start. We feel a certain way when we're with them and perceive something very familiar about that person we're attracted to, which we may interpret as being "in love." This was addressed in the previous chapter on family of origin. However, it's also associated with attraction and, consequently, has a significant impact on our choices.

Understanding our attractions and what they are about is essential to getting into the right groove for finding suitable partners. As we know by now, the area is complex and sometimes doesn't make much sense. Nothing is entirely predictable, which is why it's so important to do our individual work and get to know someone properly. It's not safe to go by our initial attractions and put too much hope on that. We need to look beyond first impressions and get to know what the person is really about. We also need to know ourselves and what we want and need before getting too established in any relationship.

If you're reading this and feeling sad or cheated about your own situation, take heart because this book was written for you. You can overcome any circumstances, no matter what childhood or former bad relationships you experienced. Always remember that knowledge is power! It's all about knowing, understanding, and becoming aware of our circumstances and the things we need to avoid. When we become aware of our vulnerabilities, it is much easier to identify those areas of naivety and deal with them more effectively. It's when we are unaware that we have a bigger chance of repeating history and continuously finding ourselves in damaging relationships. When we know about our attractions, our awareness is activated, and we can learn about the tools we need to help us make better choices moving forward.

Optional Exercises

The following suggestions aim to help you identify the patterns in your attractions to others. Stay honest with yourself as you consider the attractions that may have influenced you in the past. Or if you are new to relationships, take note of what things draw your attraction.

Things to Ponder

- What am I initially attracted to in a person?
- Have I found my initial attractions to be misleading in the past?

- How does my role in my family of origin affect my attractions?
- Why do I think I am attracted to a certain type of person?
- How does my sense of self affect my attractions?
- In what ways do I see I am vulnerable in making decisions about partners?
- In reflection, what aspects in relationships have worked best for me in the past?

Things I Can Do

- Reflect on the things that have influenced my attractions to past partners.
- Make a mind map that highlights my attraction history.
- Ask myself the what and why questions regarding my attractions.
- Make a commitment to myself to know someone properly before I commit to him or her.
- Identify any characteristics I have that make others think they can take advantage of me.
- Do further work on my sense of self if needed.

CHAPTER 14

ATTACHMENT STYLES

Understanding our own attachment style enhances our discernment.

Attachment theory is well researched in the psychology field, with continued work having extended over several decades. We know, for example, that at the basis of developmental attachment theory there are three main attachment styles. These are anxious resistant, anxious avoidant, and secure attachments. They were initially formulated by Mary Ainsworth and John Bowlby in the early 1970s. Bowlby thoroughly explains their theory in his book *A Secure Base*, which has been extremely popular in the mental health field in most parts of the world for many years. Childhood attachment theory has been further developed since its beginning by researchers such as Dan Siegel, Pat Crittenden and others, who have collectively advanced our understanding of attachment styles.

For the purpose of our relationship journeys, we will take a slightly different perspective on attachment theory. The perspective that applies to adults and our romantic relationships is better known as adult attachment theory. This helps us to identify our unique attachment styles and allows us to explore how different combinations of attachment styles interact with each other. This becomes quite valuable when we're learning to become more discerning about choosing compatible partners.

The following brief descriptions are taken from Levine and Hellers' book *Attached*, which explores the science of adult attachment to help us better understand the nature of relationships according to our unique attachment styles. Understanding how this works may provide some insights and help you to identify your attachment style.

When considering attachment styles in relationships, the different combinations are viewed in pairs as they apply to the different couple combinations. These attachment combinations will add to your ability to become more discerning in your selection of a mate. This knowledge will guide you toward understanding your attachment style and how it may have caused previous relationships to result in disappointments. It also provides guidance for improving and overcoming poor attachment connections and for knowing when it's time to leave a relationship if that's what is needed. For more in-depth information, you may want to put *Attached* on your reading list. However, for this purpose, I will attempt to explain how attachment styles affect relationships on a most basic level.

Those who have an anxious attachment style are likely to be more emotionally invested in their relationships than the average individual.

They generally yearn for closeness and need ongoing reassurance from their partners on many levels. Sometimes this is apparent to others, and the person can be seen as being needy in the relationship. This may be viewed by others as being demonstrative of an unhealthy relationship. However, this is apparently not the case, as things can change over time. The couple can develop a mutual trust, allowing the partners to build a healthier connected relationship.

Common sense tells us that every relationship requires some level of dependency on each other. This can develop into a co-dependent relationship if there's an imbalance between the couple, creating inequality. However, as anxious couples get to know each other, they generally gravitate to a healthy relationship that includes both connectedness and independence, a condition I prefer to call being interdependent. As a relationship continues, there's a need to rely on each other to do things for the common good of the couple. This comes down to compatibility and the ability to work together to bring the relationship into harmony. However, it doesn't always start off this way as the couple gets to know each other. It really depends on how the relationship progresses over time.

Anxiously attached people tend to put their partners on pedestals and hold them in high regard. Their anxiety heightens when they're away from their partners, and they can remain anxious until their return. They may hold the belief that this is their only chance of love and consequently become hypervigilant about making sure it succeeds. If anxiously attached people have low self-esteem, they can undeservedly accept blame for things, mostly to keep the peace. They can make false assumptions about what's happening in difficult times, fearing the worst. The anxiety is likely to have them settle for what they know rather than risk ending the relationship for fear of being alone. They're more likely to dismiss problems they see in their partners, mistakenly and secretly hoping they will change.

The avoidant attachment people tend to need their space and don't like to be locked in relationships that require too much ongoing closeness and intimacy. They are less likely to return phone calls and more likely to space out connections in the early days of the relationship. They may find things wrong with their partners and talk themselves into thinking it won't work, consequently ending relationships before they have a chance of survival. They tend to like more alone time and prefer their own spaces than being too connected with another. They are less likely to commit and initially may be very slow at being available in the relationship. If the relationship survives, they may avoid professing their love to their partners and can engage in flirtatious behaviours with others.

If the relationship continues past the beginning stage, avoidant attached people will tend to put a wedge between themselves and their partners. And when things look as though they're getting too close, they're more likely to cause an argument or find a way to withdraw from the relationship. As mentioned previously, they tend to find faults in their partners, and they keep score, thus driving a further wedge into the relationship. They will often seek partners who are unavailable, so they can keep their independence and avoid the true intimacy that is required for a good relationship. They will also at times take up partners from their pasts and reignite the flame in the older relationships.

In contrast to the other two attachment styles, securely attached people tend to behave in ways that bring peace and harmony to their relationships. They communicate more effectively and are less likely to engage in outbursts of anger over differences of opinion or choices regarding decisions that need to be made. Being less threatened, they do not act in defensive ways but are more likely to stay calm and talk things through. They are more comfortable being close and intimate with their partners and to show more empathy in being responsive to the needs of the other. They treat their partners with love and respect. They have more confidence in their relationships than those with anxious and avoidant attachment styles. They are also more likely to respond positively to differences, assuming their partners to have the best of intentions, thereby being quick to forgive and avoiding blame. Rather, they are more intent on keeping harmony in the relationship.

When it comes to relationships, of course, each partner has his or her individual relationship style, forming any combination of two out of the three attachment styles. For relationships in which both partners have an anxious attachment style, they can work toward developing a more secure attached relationship as they learn to know and understand each other, building the trust that is needed to be in a more secure relationship. This can also be attained through observing others who have more secure relationships and making the necessary adjustments to improve their own relationship.

The most problematic combination in attachment styles is the anxious avoidant combination, where one partner has an anxious attachment style, and the other has the avoidant. In such cases, the dance that happens between each partner is a continuous push-and-pull situation that gives out all the wrong messages, thereby preventing the relationship from flourishing. The anxious attached person continuously seeks that special person he or she sees as being "the one." The avoidant partner is threatened by any signs of intimacy, wanting to preserve his or her independence, and puts obstacles in the way to keep the distance needed for survival. This escalates with the waiting time generated by the avoidant partner, causing the anxious one to misinterpret the longing as being in love.

The dance goes on, with the self-protective, hurtful behaviour of the avoidant partner to be excused by the anxious one and dismissed as being unimportant compared to the perceived love they feel for each other. Any blaming from the avoidant partner to create distance creates an opportunity for the anxious attached person to engage in self-blaming. This can lead to "gaslighting," a situation where the offender blames the partner for his or her own poor behaviour. The excuses are escalated by the anxious partner as he or she further loses the authentic sense of self by engaging in self-loathing thoughts, feelings, and actions. The avoidant partner then works harder at balancing the need to maintain the distance necessary for perceived safety and protection. The anxious partner continues to maintain the belief of being in love, thus remaining trapped in the relationship.

You may be reflecting on your past relationships and are able to identify patterns that have caused distress. You may even be able to identify exactly how things went wrong and how attachment styles played a part. When approaching the business of choosing a partner from an attachment theory perspective, we can look at our own attachment styles and see what is needed to develop a more secure attachment style in our relationships. The combination of having a healthy sense of self and developing personal growth places us in a great position for being more secure within ourselves and will, in turn, help us to find a relationship that's based on secure attachment principles.

Because you have spent time working on your sense of self—including building your self-esteem, embracing your true character, and getting to know yourself better—you'll be well equipped to look at your attachment style. You will have gained a better understanding of how you've allowed yourself to be treated in past relationships, including how you've treated yourself. You can now reflect on your attachment style and consider the role this may have played in those relationships. This, in turn, allows you to figure out how your authentic self needs to fit into a healthy, secure relationship. It needs to be a relationship with a safe and secure foundation, at least with the potential to build the trust that's needed for a healthy connection that is able to endure over time.

You may have heard people say, as I have many times, that when they get into a relationship they change for the worse. Some say that they don't like themselves when they're in a relationship, so they're better off staying single. Understanding how attachments work in relationships provides, at least in part, an explanation as to why this may happen. The more self-aware we are, the more secure we become. Once this security becomes established, we are less likely to become trapped in unhealthy relationships and more likely to be successful in finding and keeping healthy connections.

Optional Exercises

The following exercises are to help you identify your own attachment style, and if you are in a relationship, the style of your partner and your relationship attachment pattern. You may find ways to improve your connection or do some extra work in this area if needed.

Things to Ponder

- What do I think my attachment style is?
- What do I think my relationship attachment style is?
- Do I recognise attachment patterns in previous relationships?
- Do I recognise any avoidant patterns in myself or my partner?
- Do I allow myself to be manipulated in relationships?
- Do I feel secure, and can I be myself in my relationship?

Things I Can Do

- Consider any changes I may need to make in my approach to relationships.
- If I want to understand more on attachment, read *Attached*, by Levine and Heller.
- Make a commitment to speak my truth and be honest in my relationship.
- Address avoidance behaviours if necessary.
- Work on developing a more secure approach to my relationships.
- Recognise obstacles to having a secure attachment, and discuss these with my partner.
- Seek therapy if I am in a difficult situation and need support.

CHAPTER 15

COMPATIBILITY

Some things really matter in relationships, and compatibility is a star feature!

When we first meet someone, we can be quite oblivious of the need to know whether we are going to be compatible with that person. Sometimes this is not such a big deal. After all, we need to give ourselves time to get to know them, right? After reading the previous chapters, you will be well aware of the difficulties we can get ourselves into by misreading the attraction or misunderstanding the mutual commitment to the relationship. We're generally too caught up in the moment to worry about such things. This is fine and normal in the dating game. However, it's worthwhile having an idea in your head about what you want from a relationship beforehand. This is especially important if you happen to have an anxious attachment style, or your sense of self is still on the vulnerable side.

After reading the first part of this book, you will have hopefully gained a refreshing, new perspective of yourself and have a better understanding of what's important to you in life. This is an essential requirement before you can even look at the whole notion of compatibility. Only by knowing ourselves can we start working out what type of people we need to be with to form compatible relationships. It's necessary to understand our own personality and know the things that make us happy and the things we don't like before we can decide what we need in a relationship. Sometimes this happens automatically and unfolds as couples get to know each other. However, if we have a poor relationship history and our radars are off, we can fail to see what is needed for a compatible relationship for ourselves, even though we may be able to see it in others.

We have all heard those comments about other couples such as, "They are so great together!" or, "They bring out the best [or the worst] in each other." People seem to notice if there's an authentic connection in couples, and it's great to see when people have chosen well. I remember contemplating this in the past, when I was involved in earlier relationships and wondering what made some people's relationships so great while mine struggled. This was especially true when I was young, and it was so evident that some of my friends and extended family members had such great relationships that seemed to really work well. Since then, I've learned there are many reasons why relationships work well, and compatibility is definitely a star feature.

Compatibility is an aspect of relationships that is sometimes misunderstood, so it's important to know what it really means. One common misunderstanding about compatibility is that couples should be the same type of person, who like and dislike all the same things in life. Although it's good to have things in common, this is not exactly true. When two people are too much alike, they have the potential to clash in many areas of their lives. This can cause more problems than it's worth. And while the relationship can initially seem like it's really going somewhere, after a while, the wheels can start to fall off when the constant clashing and lack of balance in the relationship becomes apparent. For example, it can get pretty volatile if both want to call the shots all the time and be in charge of the decision-making. Of course, this can be resolved if the couple does some work on it, which will lead them toward talking it through and striking a balance in the relationship. However, this requires some honest effort and compromising from both partners.

Another misconception is that couples need to be the opposite of each other. While that saying, "Opposites attract," may be true in some cases, couples who are too different from each other can get into more obvious incompatibility problems. They may find they can't agree on anything and have difficulties in making decisions together. This can also lead to arguments as they want opposite outcomes from each other, which can lead to the conclusion that the relationship is just not working. Until that time, they can develop negative feelings towards each other as incompatibility issues escalate. They are likely to want very different things, both on a daily basis and for the longer term, raising dissatisfaction in the relationship. Having different values is a common problem in relationships and often overlooked during the early stages, causing unresolvable problems down the track.

Much of this is not so evident when couples first start getting together, which means it could do with considerable thought. The extremes of being too alike and totally different don't create the most compatible couple. Compatibility is about finding the right balance between being similar and having those unique differences that express each partner's individuality. This is reflected in the theories and models on healthy couple and family functioning that have been developed through years of research. Signs of healthy functioning include a combination of togetherness with some individuality mixed into the equation. You could also phrase this as connectedness and independence. Either way, it means that to maximise compatibility, we need to strike a balance between having some similarities and being able to express our own uniqueness. This is what keeps relationships connected and interesting, and more likely to survive for the long haul.

There are certain areas in which having similarities is most important. For example, sharing similar core values is important as they are more internalised and entrenched, making them less likely to change over time. Our values are generally at the cores of our being and are such important parts of who we are. They express our authenticity, something that is important to nurture and protect as we journey through life. Shared beliefs can also be important in a relationship and certainly enhance compatibility. However, many couples have managed well with respect to having different spiritual or religious beliefs, as long as there is a genuine respect for each other's preferred belief orientation and practices.

Having similar values and beliefs regarding loyalty in the relationship is especially important. Some have become involved with partners who are unable to stay faithful and will quietly have affairs or even multiple partners on the side, sometimes over long periods of time. Apart from my experiences, I have listened to many people, mostly women and some men, over the years who have shared similar stories. This becomes extremely painful when the truth eventually comes out, causing intense grief and an overwhelming sense that they've wasted years of their lives. This causes severe emotional distress, often in both partners, not only the one who was deceived. Those who were cheated on often say that if they knew sooner, they might have had a chance to find a better life elsewhere. It can take a long time to heal. Some people never do.

Fidelity and honesty are values that need to be addressed early in the relationship, before it becomes too serious. It needs to be done sincerely and with a contingency plan if values change along the way. Honesty in relationships often falls down when it comes to affairs. The cheating partner can carry on living in two worlds, while the one being cheated on is often oblivious. The partner being cheated on has a right to know, so he or she can make a decision about what to do. I am constantly astounded by how the offending partner will downplay the affair like it's not a big deal. But it really is a major wound to the partner as the trust and belief in the relationship are violated. It takes a lot of work to restore such injuries in a relationship, and in many cases, it never happens. Honesty is important, and we need the ability to share openly our true core values about how we want to live our lives. This means being upfront for those who are aware they are unable to stay faithful.

Compatibility doesn't mean that both partners have to come from a similar family background. But it does mean they need to come to a place of shared beliefs about what is important in life. We all take on different belief systems based on what we've learned in our families of origin. This sometimes takes on a similar theme, while other times, it goes in the opposite direction. In other words, some people will go out of the way to do the opposite of how they were raised because of undesirable outcomes caused by their parents' decisions. Compatibility needs to be more about what each person believes is important and aligns with what they both desire moving forward. This will often gravitate into consideration of parenting issues once the couple has its own family, and being on the same page makes life a lot easier when raising children.

Considering spirituality is another important issue and is something that can change over time. Some people don't give this area much thought when they start their families, and then somewhere down the track, they realise their children will never learn about spiritual beliefs unless they are exposed to them. Some say things like, "They can make up their own minds when they grow up." I think this is very true and a good value to hold. However, it's also true that if children are not exposed to any kind of spiritual beliefs, they may not have the awareness to later make those choices. This doesn't necessarily mean you need to join a religious organisation, but having an open mind about spirituality and having discussions about a belief in a higher power can be helpful in the early stages of a relationship, so there is room for future conversations about the topic.

Sharing interests can in some ways make life easier, though as mentioned previously, it's not a great idea to get into the habit of doing everything together. While it's fun to enjoy many of the same things, it is so important that we don't ever lose ourselves in the process of our relationship journey. We owe it to ourselves and to those around us to express our unique individuality throughout our lives. This is what helps us to stay true to ourselves. We need to recognise our rights to express individuality and equally acknowledge our partners' uniqueness. This means that each partner needs to know he or she are free to explore and develop individual interests. When each person's individual needs are recognised, there is a mutual respect and understanding of how those respective interests matter to each other. This serves to deepen the love and respect couples have for each other.

When couples are getting to know each other, compatibility issues should be explored from the start, so there is a shared understanding of each other's expectations. It's important to give each other time and space to adjust to the relationship from the single lifestyle. This will help to avoid complaints from your friends about you not having time for them now that you're in a relationship. How many times does that happen? I'm sure you're no stranger to such comments; I have certainly heard it on numerous occasions. The last thing you want to do is abandon your friends. Our friends play important roles in our lives as they are in our lives for a reason. Whether we know it or not, our friends contribute significantly to our personal development. We talk to them about things we don't talk to anyone else about, and they will sometimes point out things to us that we can't see. Therefore, we want them around when we are cultivating new relationships.

Optional Exercises

The following suggested tasks are designed to help you work out your compatibility needs and what you are looking for in a partner. This should help you on your journey and enable you to readily identify whether something is going to work for you.

Things to Ponder

- What are my true core values?
- What other things are important to me?
- What similarities do I want to attract in a partner?
- What things are unique to me that I want to do independently?
- What value do I place on my current friendships?
- Do I stay true to myself in relationships?

Things I Can Do

- Start a new page in my journal about what my values may be in a relationship.
- Think of conversations I may be able to have with my present or future partner.
- Review past relationships to identify what was present and absent regarding compatibility.
- Make sure compatibility issues are addressed in future relationships.
- Keep a balanced perspective regarding compatibility.
- Make a commitment to myself that I will never lose myself in a relationship.

CHAPTER 16

KNOWLEDGE, POWER, AND INTUITION

Knowledge is power, and intuition is the booster.

Now that you've read about how our relationships are influenced, I'm sure you may be interested in knowing how you can attract the right kind of relationship. We've been learning how many of the problems we have in life have a pattern, and they are that way because we are creatures of habit and get used to what is comfortable. We like to do what's familiar and tend to react to anything that is different from what we are accustomed to, so the thought of getting out of our comfort zones is sometimes quite a challenge. This means if you have a history of failed relationships, you need to get out of your relationship comfort zone, and embrace the idea of being uncomfortable in this area of your life. At least until you sort things out, so they are working for you rather than against you.

It might be worthwhile to know you are not alone in this matter. There are many people in the same boat. And if you do have a pattern of getting into bad relationships, please understand that it does not necessarily make the other person bad. Most times it just means that it wasn't a good fit. People are different in different relationships, and sometimes when people separate and re-partner, they are more compatible and much happier in their new relationships though their former ones may have been fraught with problems. There are times when we stay in relationships for the wrong reasons, and this can be to everyone's detriment, including our own. So, while we're navigating new relationships, it's best not to get caught up in the blame and shame game, which is a waste of our energy. Keep moving on in our lives, and make sure we keep our minds clear about what we need to do moving forward.

There's a very simple procedure for dealing with this problem of having a troubled relationship pattern, and the same principles apply to everyone. If you can relate to this concept, you may benefit from adhering to the following formula. First, go back to your exercise in chapter 2, where I suggested you start writing a full description of yourself. This is the one that you started with, "I am," and then listed all your characteristics. If you want, you can revise your list. Seek input from others if needed to refresh your mind with all the characteristics that describe who you are. Remember to keep things positive. Then write down some of the things you love about yourself and then some things you're not so crazy about and could do with some improvement. This is a good opportunity to take time to appreciate your uniqueness and reflect on some of the work you did in part 1 of this book.

It is also an opportunity for you to reality test and consolidate what you have come to know about yourself. You can see how real things are for you, and recognise when others say nice things about you. Check in with yourself about how much you believe what's been brought to your attention. If you've struggled with having a poor sense of self for most of your life, you may find it challenging to hear nice things about yourself and now recognise an internal pattern of automatically dismissing them. Make sure you stop yourself from doing that. Think about why people are saying those positive things about you. Look for examples in your past that give evidence to those positive comments. Don't ignore them; embrace and own them. Say them out loud to yourself and add, "Yes, that's me!" or, "Yes, that is really who I am!" You can consolidate your sense of self, embrace it, own it, and enjoy being in your own goodness.

Once you're satisfied that this is in place, the next step is to ask yourself, "Knowing me the way I do, what sort of person do I need to be with to maintain my sense of self and share a happy and meaningful life?" Then start another list, one that describes the type of person you know you need to have in your life for a full and satisfying relationship. This takes a lot of thought and requires that you spend considerable time thinking about those things that are important for you to have in a partner. Don't skimp on this part of the process. Some things on your list will be not negotiable, while others will be not so important, and you can be more flexible. Some things may need to be similar, while other things can be complementary.

For example, you're going to prefer someone with personal values that are similar to your own and mark them non-negotiable and similar. You may be a bit of an introvert and may see the need to have someone in your life who is more outgoing to balance things out and help you to enjoy a more fulfilling social life. However, you won't want someone who wants to party all the time when you don't enjoy parties at all. If you have a hobby or interest that takes up a chunk of your time, you many need to consider that you need someone who also has healthy interests outside the relationship. So, you get the idea? Make sure you put heaps of effort into all the aspects of your ideal relationship. Become accustomed to knowing what you're looking for.

While you're getting on with your life and undertaking this important life-changing exercise, take notice of the types of people you come across and feel a strong attraction towards. But don't allow yourself to be swept away by the attraction. Remember to ask yourself what it's about. Take a silent inventory of their personalities, how they live their lives, what they value, what you see in them that's familiar. Try to identify what the attraction is about. Some of these strong initial attractions are likely to be misleading, which I mentioned previously. Remember that it's the early attraction that can so easily get us into trouble. They can often be extremely strong, so they can easily catch you off guard if you're not taking notice of what's really going on for you.

I strongly recommend you're diligent about this and exercise as much self-control as you need not to get caught up in a romantic whirlwind. Instead, take notice of your authentic self, based on the work you've done on yourself, and identify the qualities you're looking for in a partner. Let that be your guide! Let it replace the attractions you may notice that could lead you into another problem relationship. I've known many people to have aha moments at this stage of the process. I've also experienced this myself when doing my own hard work on gaining insights into my attractions. I was astonished at what I noticed about myself, even when my logical brain was so clearly making things apparent. It was only when I kept clear-headed, without becoming involved, that things changed, and what I was attracted to started to change dramatically. But it did take time.

Another thing that can often get us into trouble is getting too intimate too soon. Once we become intimate with someone, we may become emotionally attached. And because of the strong emotions we've created, it can become difficult to be objective about the relationship and bring it to an end if that's what we've come to understand is needed. People are different in this way. While some people can be intimate with multiple people over a relatively short period without too much concern, others are not comfortable with having multiple partners. For some people, once they become intimate with others, the thought of leaving them and starting over with someone else becomes stressful. Therefore, this is best avoided and managed differently.

I'm aware that many who are reading this will understand this predicament, so you may want to take notice of where you stand on this matter. For the sake of this initiative, if you're on this journey after having many problem relationship experiences, I recommend you slow things down a bit. This is not a quick fix but a part of your journey, and it requires your attention to be mindful of what you need to do. You can educate yourself to help you achieve your goals, so take it easy, be kind to yourself, and don't be in a hurry. Let yourself be guided in your journey, and learn as much as you can along the way.

This is a good time to remind you that this is not a slam dunk! It is not a 100 percent guaranteed formula to find and land your ideal mate. There is no such thing in existence. Rather, it's a procedure that you can follow to get out of your old pattern and start to be more discerning about who you invite or allow into your life. You will be more ready to act quickly and avoid becoming too involved with potential partners when you see some of the old signs showing themselves. This is a way for you to have a much better chance of finding someone who's a good match for you and form a relationship that results in you creating a better life for yourself by choosing wisely.

The feedback I've received regarding the success of this formula over a long period is substantial. Though I don't claim a perfect success rate, I know it has worked for many people, and I am confident it will continue to do so. It may take a few relationships, hopefully brief ones, doing some necessary exploration in the dating game while you work out what's happening in your unique situation. However, it will be well worth the effort!

Another important reminder on this topic: If we want to be successful in life, we need to learn how to let go of things that are not working for us and move on. Remember that we will do best when we focus our energy on what we have power over, letting go of all the rest. With relationships, our power is about what or who we allow to come into our lives and what we do with situations when they present themselves to us. We need to keep this in mind so that we stay empowered and don't ever allow ourselves to give that power away. If someone is behaving towards us in a way that is demeaning or doesn't have our best interests at heart, then it's time to say goodbye and move on. In doing so, we maintain our power and don't give it to anyone else. We never have to put up with partners who treat us disrespectfully in any way. We need to remember that we have the power to never allow that to happen. We will be more attuned to this if it has happened in the past..

After giving this process considerable time to work through your personal issues, your intuition will hopefully become more in tune with what you want to achieve. For example, you may start to notice at some point that you're looking at people differently, noticing the differences between your former attractions and the things that are becoming more appealing to you now. This is when you know you've made significant progress on this journey. It will become more noticeable as you spend more time with like-minded people. You may realise that you've developed a sixth sense for noticing different aspects of people's personalities. You can use your intuition to guide you and make sure you don't settle for less than what you know will be good for you. You call the shots regarding what's right for you!

Optional Exercises

These suggestions will help you to connect with some of the earlier things you learned about yourself, solidify your sense of self, and remind you of your need to continue working on gaining and maintaining empowerment in your life.

Things to Ponder

- Have I taken on board the things that I learned about myself in the previous chapters?
- What have I learned about myself since?

- What am I understanding now that I wasn't taking on board earlier?
- How can I stop myself from following through with familiar attractions?
- What prompts can I put in place to stay true to myself?
- Where is my power in my current situation?

Things I Can Do

- Write a detailed description of the attributes I need in a partner.
- Work out a plan for how I may slow things down in new relationships.
- Write myself an alert list of things that may trap me in future relationships.
- Journal how I see my empowerment so far on my relationship journey.
- Journal my thoughts about my intuition unfolding and becoming apparent.
- Practice using my intuition in my life, especially in my relationship journey.

CHAPTER 17

SETTING YOUR INTENTION

Believe in yourself ... engage your imagination ... set your intention!

Now that you've discovered a whole lot of information about yourself in your relationship journey, both personally and in the history of your previous relationships, you will most likely be aware that the next step is how to achieve the desires of your heart. I hope you've succeeded in learning how to love and appreciate yourself in the most authentic way, worked out the nature of your personal attractions, and discovered the type of partner you really want and need. After all this great work, you will want to make things go in your favour. You will want to start testing the waters, so to speak, to check how your attractions are changing and noticing the differences in how you approach the whole world of relationships. Those things you've figured out so impressively need to continue educating you in some way, so you can eventually have the kind of relationship you are really looking for and that will bring you the happiness you deserve.

A word of wisdom is needed here. This is not about creating a happy, fairy-tale ending, something you may have stored in the back of your mind for many years. It may not be your Prince Charming image that you captured from watching fairy tales and reading romance novels. This is life, and we need to prepare to be realistic. We're talking about putting into action a process that minimizes the chances of having misleading attractions and maximizes the chances of finding someone who can lead you towards a much happier life. It's about finding a relationship that works well for two people, and it requires patience as you give the principles time to work. There's also a need to stay in a place of willingness to continue learning and gaining a better understanding of yourself along the way. You will need to test yourself at times, especially when you feel attracted to someone, to see whether the attraction has you following your old pattern, or if there's something new and inspirational happening that may feel somewhat unfamiliar.

By the time you are at this point, if you've done some of the exercises and taken up the challenges along the way, you are likely to have a pretty good idea of what you want to achieve. That is, you will know what type of relationship you want, what type of person you are looking for, some things about the person's personality, a lot more about the person's values, and have an idea of the potential partner's belief system. You also may have an idea about some of the interests you would particularly like the individual to have if that's something important to you. Alternatively, you may require the individual to have more interests of his or her own, independent of you. Whatever the case, you will have a much clearer idea about what you want than when you started reading this book.

Setting our intentions encompasses many facets, some of which were addressed earlier in this book. It's about knowing without a doubt that we have the right to have a happy and fulfilling relationship and to believe that it will actually happen. It's about putting ourselves in a certain space, one of total belief that allows us to know we can have those things our hearts desire. However, there are times when the biggest challenge for this is our need to believe in ourselves as individuals with something to offer and that we can attract special people into our lives. This is why the work on yourself is so important on this relationship journey. We will have a lot of trouble being happy with others in our lives if we are not satisfied and fully accepting of ourselves in all our imperfections.

One of the most self-defeating mistakes I've seen people make is the inability or unwillingness to believe they can have happy and fulfilling relationships. This can be due to their ongoing disbelief in themselves or that because of past mistakes, they are not capable of having the relationships they desire. In some cases, they've never had a relationship, and as time goes on, the disbelief becomes more established. This always puzzles me, especially when I see beautiful young women and handsome young men who are incredibly lovely people who have never had a relationship. There are different reasons for this, from extreme shyness to low self-esteem to not having the opportunities to meet people. In such cases, the longer it goes on, the more hope is lost, and the less likely it is that those people can believe in finding true love in their lives.

In his book *The Power of Intention,* Dr. Wayne Dyer talks about, "giving forth what you want to attract." This well-known principle is common to many inspirational belief systems. In this particular context, it makes sense that if we want to attract others with certain qualities and values, then we need to portray those qualities and values ourselves. Dyer named this a, "universe of attraction and energy." And like other esteemed colleagues in the field of neuroscience and quantum physics, this gives evidence to an energy field that works amongst and around us. Dr. Joe Dispenza explains how this is activated through our creative energy, based on our intentions, combined with passions or heightened emotions behind that intention. That is, when we visualise what we want to attract and combine this with passion, emotion, and inspiration, we can attract that thing we desire to ourselves. Apparently, this universal principle applies whether negative or positive, so it's most important that we keep our mindsets in a positive frame and practice focusing on what we want, not on what we don't want. It means breaking free from negativity!

Let's ask the question, "What are the obstacles that keep us from linking into our power of intention?" Slipping back into self-doubt is our number-one enemy. We cannot afford to allow self-doubt to come into the equation when we're on the path of intention. Self-doubt is the opposite of self-confidence and works against our abilities to believe in ourselves and to achieve those outcomes we've set out in our minds to accomplish.

Another obstacle is giving up too soon. We can become impatient, expecting to see results "yesterday." This process requires self-discipline, the ability to trust in the process and see it through. A good way to look at this is, "It will eventuate when the time is right." The best thing you can do is get on with the job of being yourself, and continue with your personal growth. This time provides a window for you to develop yourself further before your relationship begins.

Another obstacle that's become apparent is that some people think they must be stunningly gorgeous to be in the running to have a relationship. This is simply not true! People come in all varieties, their looks, personalities, heights, weights, and everything else. While it is true that there are some aesthetically beautiful people in the world, not everyone is going to look like a movie star or a model. In fact, there are many people who would not be described by some as being really attractive, yet are in wonderful, happy, and connected relationships. It's not all about looks and achievements. It's about compatibility and the mutual suitability between two people. Everyone deserves to find love, and I believe there is someone for everyone if that's what you want. And remember that famous saying, "Beauty is in the eye of the beholder."

You may notice other obstacles getting in the way of believing you can attract the right person and have a meaningful relationship. I think it's wise to check with yourself to see if there is something standing in the way, or maybe there are issues fuelling your self-doubt. If you think that's happening for you, make sure you confront it and deal with it so you can let it go. Allow yourself to be free of all obstacles—including self-doubt, impatience, negative self-beliefs, poor self-concepts, or anything else—that may be standing in the way. Talk to someone, think it through, pray for guidance, journal it. Do whatever it takes to make a clear pathway to move on with your intention. Develop a steadfast belief that you can have a great relationship with a wonderful person who is exactly the right fit for you. Then when you meet and get to know that person, in time you will develop an inner-knowing that this is the one for you. That is your intuition at work. And it goes beyond the head and heart levels, giving you a wonderful sense of calm.

An excellent way to set our intentions and bring about what we want and need in our lives is to engage in meditation. Using a simple mindfulness meditation to bring your whole being into a state of calmness is a good start. Engage your imagination by allowing yourself to visualise your life how you want it to be. Let your creative mind flow and energise your thoughts further. Tap into all your senses so that you can see, feel, hear, smell, and imagine touching what you want to come forth into your life. This is something we need to experience rather than just read or talk about, so it's best to put these principles into practice and start doing them every day, even if it's something unfamiliar to you. I've had some of my most inspirational moments after doing meditations as a space seems to emerge that gives me guidance and direction that I don't know I would have received otherwise. I highly recommend this practice to everyone.

Another important point on this topic is to watch what you say and how you think as you go about the business of life. This helps to ensure all aligns with your intention and what you are believing. Numerous spiritual teachers and leaders constantly emphasise the importance of minding what we say and how we think. Those things we feed to our minds will strongly influence our beliefs and actions. We tend to own our beliefs, accept them as being the way things are, and everything that happens is interpreted through our belief systems. It's like the engine that drives the machine, so it's important that we guard our thoughts and words because that will determine what we bring into our lives. This is why positive affirmations can be effective. These positive words are instilled to replace negative thoughts with the intention of shifting entrenched negative belief systems.

With this in mind, you may like to check how you think about yourself and your situation, and what you say to yourself. If you find you engage in a lot of negative self-talk, you can take action by replacing the negative words with positive ones. For example, instead of saying things like, "I can't see this ever eventuating into anything," or, "This is taking too long," speak in line with what you're working towards, such as, "I'll meet my person at exactly the right time, and meanwhile, I'm grateful for who I am and what I have already." You can make up your own positive affirmations based on your current negative thought patterns by identifying the opposite of how you're thinking. Ask yourself, "What's a more positive way of looking at this?"

I hope you are having more "aha" moments as the light shines on those things that need attention in your thought life. When the light comes on, the darkness disappears! Speak words of gratitude and abundance to bring about your desired outcome. Stay positive, and just get on with enjoying your life as, "It may happen when you least expect it!"

Optional Exercises

The following exercises are designed to help you to develop your mindset so that you can stay in a positive frame of mind when you want to attract someone into your life. It may be foreign, but it is well worth exploring new ways that are uplifting for your soul.

Things to Ponder

- How much do I really understand about meditation?
- Do I see myself as being an intuitive person?
- Can I see myself with the relationship I want?
- Do I need to remove self-doubt and develop my belief in myself?
- Have I given enough consideration to the power of intention in my life?
- What needs to change in what I say and the way I think about myself?
- Do I need to read further afield to learn more about how to achieve what I want?

Things I Can Do

- Complete any exercises I may have missed but now see that I need to do.
- Practice visualisation to strengthen this skill as if it were a muscle.
- Strengthen my intuition by taking more notice of my internal gut instincts.
- Practice positive affirmations to replace negative thoughts and beliefs.

- Practice daily meditation for at least ten minutes (best in the morning).
- Practice creative activities to develop my creative mind and enhance visualisation skills.
- Read a recommended book if I need to learn more about setting my intention.

CHAPTER 18

YOUR SOUL PURPOSE

Finding your soul purpose is the biggest reward on your life journey!

In chapter 8, I introduced the notion that there's more to life than what we see and hear, and that we are spiritual beings having a human experience. I also mentioned how many people already know this, and in fact, all people at some level, even subconsciously, will have this in part of their awareness. Understanding this can be difficult for some people, either because they've grown up without an understanding of a spiritual world, they haven't had any spiritual experiences that they recall, they've had negative experiences with religion, or they think spirituality is a bit "woo-woo" and against science. All these reasons are perfectly understandable, though none of them rule out the possibility of a spiritual world being very real. Therefore, it's likely we may be able to receive some guidance when it comes to getting our relationships sorted.

Choosing a partner is an important decision as most people intend to have relationships that are going to survive. No one really gets into a serious relationship expecting it to only last a short time. Rather, there is more likely an expectation for that person to be around for life, or at least for a very long time. This is especially important for those who are young and want to have a family. When relationships are intended for life but break down much sooner, there is usually overwhelming distress and intense heartache. Families are pulled apart, often leaving children to struggle as they are forced to deal with the fallout that is followed by having to adjust to living in two homes, and in many cases, experiencing disharmony between their parents.

Mental health professionals and others who work with this population see first-hand the devastating effects that volatile relationship breakdowns have on all family members, but especially on the children. I understand many reasons contribute to these situations, and the break-up is often necessary due to various forms of domestic violence, betrayal, incompatibility, falling out of love, and other challenging circumstances. In previous chapters, I've talked about being attracted to someone for the wrong reasons and the need to be discerning about who we choose as our life partners. Many of us know the mess we can find ourselves in when we've gone down a path where we've chosen partners who haven't been a good fit. The evidence I have of such situations is considerable from years of experience in my work and earlier on in my research on divorce and separated families.

Let's face it, getting things right in our relationship choices is a real challenge, and one that's fraught with obstacles that lead us towards giving in to something that misleads us along the way. Engaging with our spiritual selves to assist us in our efforts in discernment will have a huge impact on this part of our journey. Seeking spiritual guidance will influence our abilities to discern, guide us in the decisions we make, and determine how the rest of our journey unfolds. Therefore, it's well worth our while to engage our spiritual selves in the pursuit of finding the partners who will be the best for us. However, while travelling this road, it pays to be aware that not everyone who comes into your life as a possible partner is necessarily meant for you long term.

I believe that in many cases, people come into our lives for a reason. Sometimes this will be because we need to learn something about ourselves from being with that person. In such circumstances, the relationship may only be meant for a season rather than the long term. Other times, you will meet that person who stands out and have an awareness that this one is meant to be there for the longer journey. So how do we tell the difference? How do we know which type of relationship this will be? The answer is that often we don't know, unless we are spiritually attuned and listening to our gut instincts. And sometimes we don't know until it's too late. This is often identified in one of those hindsight aha moments, when we may say to ourselves or anyone who wants to listen, "Why on earth didn't I see that?" or, "What was I thinking?" Well, we know that we can't always rely on early attractions, so what do we do?

The earlier chapters on working out your unique personal stories and gaining discernment in your relationship choices will give you some understanding. It will also provide guidance to help you become more aware of the difficulties you can encounter and to learn about the type of person you really want to attract. The spiritual part is about us each seeking answers about our own soul purpose in life and about asking for guidance regarding who we are meant to be with in our unique life journey. The hope that we have by reaching out to that Higher Power is that we will each find that someone who will be a good match. Of course, it works the other way around too. You will also want to be a good match for your partner to make the relationship work.

I understand that this topic differs amongst people as we all have our own belief systems and choices about what we believe. I like to look at things in more of a universal way that doesn't rely on a particular belief system such as those found in religious practices. Rather, I believe it's to our advantage that we embrace the concept of keeping an open mind about spirituality. In my own life, I have learned that having faith and trusting in that Higher Power brings incredible results. There have been many times in my life when I have sought help and received answers, even though they weren't always in ways that I had expected. Furthermore, they are not always in my own timing, which becomes more evident down the track, when looking at what has unfolded in hindsight.

Most people will admit that they believe in something other than the here and now and that there is a universal power that is able to guide us in life. I believe wholeheartedly in that universal or spiritual power and that it is always available to us, ready and willing to help each of us through our life journey. This means we can ask to be guided towards those who are meant to be in our lives and that we will cross paths with them at some point. Having faith adds a whole new dimension to the quest as we can begin to expect the right people to come into our lives at the right time.

This is difficult to explain, though it is understood through experience. Somehow, having that trust provides peace of mind, and we're less likely to stress and worry about little things not going our way. If we bring this concept of faith into our awareness, we can become more attuned to the guidance we're receiving. This powerful intelligence, whether referred to as God, the Universe, Love, our Higher Power, or whatever else we like to call it, knows better than us. We can trust that and know that we're not alone; when we reach out we are being guided.

If you're someone who believes there is something more to life than what we see—and from my experience most people do— and that there is a purpose for your life, doesn't it make sense that you would want to find yourself on the track you were destined to follow? If you can keep this in mind as you gain some insights and understanding about your relationship choices, you may start to develop more of an intuitive nature to your discerning ability. At times, this may feel like your conscience is telling you something. Looking back at the work you've done on yourself regarding your sense of self, along with all the things you've realised you need in a relationship, and asking for guidance in your quest to find that special person, how much more prepared are you to make good choices?

These days, most people seem to meet through dating websites. Although this has its setbacks with some people spouting mistruths about themselves, there are some advantages too. This is because the more aware you are of what you want and need in a relationship, the more discerning you can be, and the more successful you're likely to be in your choices from the start. When you're at the point of looking for a partner, it's time to reflect on those things that you decided earlier to put on your non-negotiable list. These are the essential things that you're looking for, not to be confused with those things that are negotiable.

By paying attention to the things that matter the most, you can avoid getting yourself into situations where you can be swept away and attracted to someone for the wrong reasons. Remember that sometimes attractions grow while you're getting to know someone. Being aware of those things that you know are important for your ongoing personal happiness and contentment, is paramount in this process. This doesn't mean that there's no need for chemistry. Of course, that's important too and we definitely want that to be a part of the deal! It's just that sometimes the evidence of that takes a little longer as it often develops when people get to know each other better. When we're on the right track, that chemistry becomes stronger through time.

When we're trying to work out our purpose in our lives, we often don't know what is in store for us, though we may have an inkling or two based on what we know at any given time of our self-discovery. The same goes for our choices in partners as we don't know exactly who we need to be with but can have an idea of what type of things we need to create and maintain a fulfilling relationship. When we each give ourselves space in our hearts to question our soul purpose, it will have an impact on what and who we attract into our lives. The partner choice is an important one, so this needs some very real attention in your prayers and meditations. It's well worth the effort because it has such a huge potential to make a difference in your life. And it certainly can't do any harm!

PART 3
MAKING YOUR RELATIONSHIP WORK

Successful long-term relationships are

created through

small words, small gestures, and

small acts.

—John M. Gottman,

Eight Dates: A Plan for Making Love Last Forever

CHAPTER 19

CREATING A HAVEN

Safety is the foundation of every successful relationship!

The remainder of this book focuses on relationship education. It will help prevent common mishaps and provide guidance towards creating a sound foundation for your relationship. This information is provided because of the large number of people who attend therapy in desperate need of help during the first few years of their relationships. However, they are not the only ones. Others who've had a succession of failed relationships will say similar things. Their comments relate to not knowing how to be in a relationship or not having the skills needed to make it work. They will say things like, "I have no idea how to have a relationship," or, "I'm terrible at relationships." Such comments are often followed by anguish about growing up in a family with poor role models. Therefore, understanding how to have a healthy relationship can be difficult, yet couples are supposed to automatically know what to do. But more often than not, they don't!

Young people especially grapple with what is acceptable and what is not in relationships. My twenty-two-year-old granddaughter was telling me recently how she overheard a young girl talking to her friends about her relationship. She was describing how she was being treated by her boyfriend, speaking to her disrespectfully, including calling her disgusting names. Apparently, the other girls were giving her advice about how to handle the situation and were saying things like, "Yeah they're like that sometimes. You just have to put up with that." My granddaughter was horrified to hear such advice coming from her friends. More than likely, peer influence would have had a role to play in how that young girl progressed with her relationship. Hopefully she got out of it before it was too late. I was most grateful that my granddaughter was able to discern that this was not okay and a really awful way to be starting off in a relationship.

Sometimes it's the other way around. I've come across women who can be rather entitled and put unreasonable demands on their partners to the point that everyone notices but the person herself. This can be difficult to watch if you're the bystander, yet the person can continue to behave unreasonably with unrealistic standards and without any awareness of the sense of entitlement. There's nothing wrong with having standards; we all need to have them. But when unrealistic expectations are combined with a lack of empathy for the partner, there is no safety in the relationship. It's also possible that the match was not a good one in the first place. Either way, this can lead to partners struggling to find safe spaces for themselves in their relationships.

I wonder sometimes how unsafe men must feel when they are

constantly under surveillance for what they are doing and saying, terrified they'll be shown up as being inadequate and not meeting their partners' needs. Unbeknown to most women, it is quite natural for decent, caring, and loving men to actually "live" to make their partners happy. For some men, nothing pleases them more! You may have heard the phrase, "Happy wife, happy life!" Well, believe it or not, some men live by this rule and are constantly doing their best to keep things running smoothly. I actually prefer the phrase, "Happy spouse, happy house!" I'm not sure where I heard this, but I'm thinking it's probably more reasonable than the former gender-specific phrase.

My partner and I have had numerous discussions about the "radical feminism" and the 'men's rights' movements. This discussion has been going on for many years as it seemed to be a feature that was evident in both our professional worlds, his as a Doctor of Philosophy in the field of social policy and mine as a Clinical Psychologist. We always came to the same conclusions from our discussions. And as you will see, it's really not rocket science! When we see things totally from an extreme feminist perspective, we will only see the interactions between men and women through female lenses. Likewise, when the men's rights' perspective dominates opinions and beliefs, we will also see things through a limited focus, this time through a male-dominant perspective. Such extremes are unbalanced and dysfunctional. They also tend to promote two sides constantly warring against each other.

When there's a clear imbalance in society, it is important that we collectively work towards creating a more harmonious equality. Because male dominance was entrenched in our society for so long, it's been necessary for the feminist movement to come alive and women's voices to be heard in order to redress this imbalance. At this time, it is relevant and necessary for women to step up and be heard in order for them to gain equality in the world and have their true worth recognised.

Just to be clear about this, in discussing these totally different perspectives, I am talking about extremes rather than the more balanced viewpoints. This is because extreme perspectives are not going to solve any problems related to cultivating real, authentic, loving relationships. We cannot have a fair and equal experience that really works when we're stuck on one side of things without being able to offer any flexibility, and especially being able to hear what's going on for the other person. This is a two-way process in which both men and women have a responsibility to respect each other's positions in life and recognising each other's strengths and potential contributions to the world.

This issue is so important as it resides at the very core of couples being able to create a haven for themselves and for each other. It must work both ways. And if we want to be heard, we need to be prepared to listen. We need to take notice of each other and care enough to make sure we are providing a safe environment, not only for ourselves, but also for our partners to enable our relationships to survive and thrive.

Relationships that work well don't generally just happen. They work because each partner has played his or her part well and been fair in their give and take with all manner of things that can happen in a relationship. This same principle applies regardless of gender, and it is just as relevant for same-sex and any other couples. However, male and female examples are given here for ease of explanation given the well-known differences in relative strengths.

In the practical sense, although there are variations to the theme, let's look at the obvious differences between men and women. Hands down, men have the physical strength. In most cases, they are built more muscularly, stronger, are able to lift and carry heavier items, can use force to open things that women sometimes struggle with, and are able to do more strenuous physical work. Men generally have the capacity to be superior in any tasks that require speed and strength. A good example of this is seen in sporting events, which are set with different achievement levels for men and women simply because of physical ability. It's not a matter of opinion; it is indeed a reality. However, this fact is only about how we are physically different and does not diminish the power of women and their strengths at all.

Women are in no way inferior, but in general, they have quite varied and different strengths. Women are more likely to have the edge over men with a range of skills, including but not limited to their language capacities, emotional intelligence, intuition, and their abilities to nurture and care for the more vulnerable family members. They are more likely to exhibit a unique wisdom that comes from being able to think things through differently than men do, and talk about those things that require understanding and interacting with more emotional intelligence. They are often able to provide guidance in various life situations, and they can be extremely good problem-solvers. For thousands of years, men have relied on the wisdom of women to help make good decisions regarding important issues. There is ample evidence of how men have sought the intuitive opinions of women to support this fact. Furthermore, women in leadership are of such immense value in our world, and this is one of the many reasons the feminist movement is active in striving to achieve equality.

Of course, this is not a black-and-white issue as there are always variations on any theme, and this one is no exception. However, this area of difference needs to be addressed because most domestic violence situations are caused by men showing their physical strength against women in horrendous ways. I don't need to get into this too deeply because we all know what I'm talking about. Men need to know their strength and take responsibility for how they use it, especially when it comes to women and children. I don't know about you, but I am really fed up with hearing about how domestic violence has played out in families. Some situations are dire, leaving women and children beaten and sometimes killed by the hands of a partner with no control over his anger. Others are more common, with women trapped in situations from which they need to flee and seek refuge.

At times, women need to take drastic measures to survive, to gain and maintain their safety while protecting their families. In doing so, they are providing role models for their sons and daughters of how important it is for partners to treat each other with respect and not tolerate abuse. Men also have a responsibility to provide good role models for their children as they are always watching how their parents are behaving. History tends to repeat itself, so parents have this responsibility and with it, opportunities to teach their children how to live with respect for themselves and others. These should be the primary goals for all adults before becoming parents and well-practiced by the time their children are born. Role modelling is one of the strongest influences on child development, and we need to do it well for the sake of our children and future generations.

The use of physical strength or psychological bullying to dominate partners or children will cause substantial damage to the relationship that may not be repairable. I urge those who have anger issues to get the professional help they need, so they can provide a safe place for their partners and current or future families. Men are wonderful and to be valued in our society. But it's so important for them to know their strength and to know when and how to use it appropriately. If you are reading this and recognise you have a problem with temper outbursts, or adult tantrums, and have a habit of acting out and apologising later, you will benefit from getting professional help. It's never okay to use your physical strength to gain supremacy over your family members, or anyone else for that matter. It does not make it okay to repeatedly become remorseful and say you're sorry later. Getting the psychological support you need for anger management is a sign of strength and will help to prevent further and possibly worse problems ahead.

Safety in relationships is as much about emotional and psychological matters as it is physical. On average, women tend to talk more than men, and this sometimes means gossiping to their girlfriends about things that should be kept between the couple. Women can also badmouth their partners and tell way too many tales out of school. This is not okay and will not contribute to creating a haven in your relationship. I understand that people will have those moments when they are at the end of their tether, when they can't get through to their partner and don't know what to do. It can be helpful to have a vent and get some advice from those you trust. But if you have a situation that's getting out of hand, you may benefit from seeking help from a professional. Don't waste time and dig your hole deeper. Do something about it, and get the help you need.

The information in this chapter applies to any gender-orientated couples as the same problems can occur that involve bullying, gossiping, and undermining patterns of behaviour. Any kind of domination or manipulation does not allow relationships to prosper. When couples engage in dysfunctional patterns of behaviour, safety in the relationship is compromised, and this rocks the whole foundation in the relationship. It's so important that regardless of what life throws our way, we keep that haven in place in our relationships so we can weather the storms together. This is how real love plays out and how we overcome any obstacles that come our way in our lives and in our relationships.

The following chapters are designed to promote healthy behaviours and attitudes in relationships. Whether you're beginning a relationship or already in one, the following chapters are packed with information that you are likely to find useful. They will either help you get things off to a good start, or if you are in a relationship, provide you with some insights that will help you to make the necessary adjustments to help you develop a happy and fulfilling relationship that is safe and loving.

Note

If you have become aware of being in a domestic violence relationship, please reach out for help. You can contact a domestic violence centre in your community, or you can seek support from trusted family members or friends. No form of domestic violence is acceptable as it's not a safe relationship. Your responsibility is towards keeping you and your children, if you have them, safe. We all have a right to feel safe in our relationships.

Optional Exercises

These suggestions are designed to help you work out a healthy formula for your relationships moving forward. Wherever you are in your journey, use these exercises as a way of forming good practices, making improvements, or changing unhelpful habits.

Things to Ponder

- Do I promote physical and emotional safety in my relationships?
- Are my expectations reasonable, or are they unrealistic?
- Do I tend to dominate some areas of my relationships?
- Do I allow my partner to dominate any aspects of my life?
- What can I do to ensure my partner feels safe?
- What can I do to ensure my own safety?
- Do I need to change any bad habits learned from my family of origin?

Things I Can Do

- Seek further education before getting into another relationship.
- Approach my relationship with an attitude of fairness and equality.
- Speak with my partner about whether we both feel safe in our relationship.

- Have a regular catch-up with my partner to clear up any issues we may have.
- Communicate with my partner regarding fairness and equality in our relationship.
- Read more self-help books on creating a healthy relationship.
- Seek professional help if needed.

CHAPTER 20

MUTUAL RESPECT AND CREATING HARMONY

Mutual respect creates harmony in our relationships.

As we all come from different families, and even though we may have similar values and belief systems, there will be significant differences in what we experienced and how we were raised. Interestingly, right, wrong, or otherwise, in the beginning of a relationship, we mostly seem to gravitate to what we know. That is, we automatically go towards whatever way we learned about all sorts of things in our daily living experiences in our families of origin. It doesn't even matter if we disliked the lifestyle of the family we came from and became aware of being raised in a dysfunctional family, we will often find ourselves automatically gravitating towards behaving in similar ways and developing the same habits of family functioning.

Many couples will battle through and eventually work it all out together, which will result in them doing things very differently. However, at the beginning of a relationship, finding your own groove and learning how to do things the way you want can be rather challenging. It takes time to gain the experience and sort it out together as a couple. And it means a lot of compromising and changing of old habits. Sadly, some never sort this one out, and it can be yet another catalyst for a breakdown in the relationship, especially when partners are stubborn and don't want to compromise.

We can only imagine what happens when two people are raised in very different ways with differences in their value systems and beliefs; attitudes towards cleanliness, tidiness, mealtimes, noisiness, bedtimes, waking times; management of finances; and in almost everything. So many changes are needed for that couple to find their own groove as a couple, and creating a harmonious solution to their different ways. Believe it or not, some couples break up over not being able to get on the same page with some of these basic life situations. They may be aggravated and put up with the discomfort of doing things against their grain for a while, but eventually, these things can take their toll. If there is no compromise or willingness to do things differently, there's going to be tension in the relationship that will eventually need managing.

This may seem less of a problem initially in the relationship but can become increasingly problematic as time goes on, especially when children come into the picture. Each partner then has to accommodate differences in parenting styles, whether they are strict, super-casual, or have more of a diplomatic style of parenting. Couples need to decide on so many things when they are raising children, and some of the issues that arise can be incredible sources of conflict. Then there's the decision-making process and how that is managed. How will you make decisions as a couple, and what will you do if you are unable to agree? These issues are best discussed earlier rather than later as it takes time and patience for us to get to know our partners and how they think or act in different situations.

Fortunately, many couples work this one out along the way and form their own ways of doing things that is different from how either of them grew up. This is what we all need to aspire to, going through enough personal growth to develop our own understandings of how we want our family life to be while accommodating the needs of all family members, including spouses and children. If this is something you have conquered in your relationship, then well done! Don't take it for granted either because this is one way in which you are contributing to creating harmony in your home. If this is ringing bells for you because it's still creating problems in your home, then it may be worthwhile taking a moment to re-evaluate your situation. Wherever you are in this process, it really isn't that difficult to make some positive changes to get things working better.

Let's say that you are challenged right now because you realise that you and your partner don't agree on a lot of the ways you're doing things in your home, and you're constantly annoyed with the outcome because it's not your way. Hmmm, it might be time to sit down together and hash things out. Having a chat can be productive when both partners are given time and space to talk about the way they grew up in their respective homes and what they value moving forward. This works best if it's done without interrupting each other. Partners can also support each other by asking further questions, such as, "What was the outcome?" "What effect did that have on you?" Do you see those things as positive or negative?" "Was there something meaningful about the way some things were done that remain special to you?" When we take the time to explore such things, it gives us opportunities to get to know our partners better and learn what makes each other tick.

You may even want to go and talk it through with a couple's therapist. This is not a bad idea as a good relationship therapist can help you towards getting on the same page. Alternatively, you could jot down some notes about the things you're learning, so you can look back on them later and see how you may be able to compromise or even come to some different solutions that you both agree on. If you have children and are experiencing conflict in the way you're raising them, then consider doing a parenting course together. This is a great way of getting both parents to think through their beliefs and parenting strategies and then navigate the path towards getting on the same page. Research in this area tells us that once parenting issues are sorted, the relationship between the couples improve, bringing harmony into the home.

If we want to have good relationships, especially if we grew up in a dysfunctional family like many of us did, it's quite important we let go of some of our preconceived ideas and stubborn beliefs. We would do well to break the habit of always thinking we know better about every situation. Just because our parents behaved in certain ways and that's what we know, it doesn't give us the right to expect our partners to fit in with our familiar ways of doing things. Nor should we expect ourselves to continue repeating unhelpful patterns. It's amazing how often this happens, even though the person may know that the parent being used as a role model caused the family distress and produced the most undesirable outcomes.

We need a reminder here that this is not an excuse to blame our parents for everything they ever did that made life hard for us. Our parents most likely did their best at the time with what they knew, given their conditions and limitations in life. Remember that blame produces a victim mentality in us. And in the process, it causes us to give away our power, making us unable to address the issue. When we recognise we've landed in a situation of history repeating itself, we have a golden opportunity to face the reality of the changes we need to make. This in turn will enable us to create new ways of doing things and put them to the test until we've achieved the best outcomes possible.

Our willingness to listen to each other respectfully and allow ourselves to compromise where necessary provides for us the potential to make some positive changes. As we dare to be different from our former selves, we are becoming courageous, and in the process, empowering ourselves and our relationships. Respecting differences in our partners has the potential to deepen relationships, and even when one partner is not on board, this has the potential to encourage a reciprocal response over time. When we can really listen to each other, exercise our empathy skills, and make an effort to understand each other, we will take our relationships to new levels. We can make positive changes that will become longstanding and prevent much anguish in the future. Through expressing our humility, we are able to make any necessary changes, and they are definitely worth the effort!

Creating harmony in a relationship through developing mutual respect does not just happen. We must work at it. There is so much wonderful information available about relationships by qualified professionals in self-help books and through other means. We can learn through materials written by relationship experts, whether supported with scientific evidence or through years of experience working with couples. As a word of caution, though, be careful who you take advice from as some well-meaning people can give advice that leaves a lot to be desired. Our relationships are too important to take notice of idle opinions, even if they are from well-meaning sources. Seek information from those who are qualified to provide the guidance you need and understand the area well as there are generally multiple issues that require consideration in most relationships.

If we want a harmonious relationship, we need to know what makes relationships work best and how things sometimes get out of hand. We can't afford to forget that dynamic phrase, "Knowledge is power," as we need this to survive in our relationship journeys. It can be easy to ignore uncomfortable things early in the relationship, but they will catch up with us if we don't address them. As you allow yourself to grow and consider your partner's needs as well as your own, you will have the opportunity to know your partner on a deeper level and enrich your relationship in the process. We can't expect to get everything right from the start as we will make mistakes. But when we take responsibility for and learn from those mistakes, we create opportunities for more harmony in our relationships.

On the topic of making mistakes, many problems are created in couples when there is an expectation for the relationship to be perfect to be acceptable. If you haven't worked this one out yet, there is no such thing as a perfect relationship. Aiming for perfection in our relationships will cause us to become easily annoyed or even offended when our partners do not do things the ways we want. We need to understand that our ways are not always the only ones leading to a solution. In fact, there are many ways to approach things or complete a task, and sometimes we need to be humble enough to sit back and allow our partners to do things how they choose. We will always have opportunities to demonstrate our own ways of doing things, and that's just another way we learn from each other.

If we struggle with perfectionism in our personal lives, it's likely this will also affect our relationships, and we will find ourselves treating our partners the same ways we've been treating ourselves possibly for most of our lives. We can't expect ourselves or our partners to get everything right, or we'll set ourselves up for continual disappointments. If we want to create and keep harmony in our relationships, we need to let go of perfectionism and embrace the concept of imperfection. Although scary, this creates a wonderful experience as we get to embrace a sense of liberation from our restricted belief systems. It's important to accept our mistakes, and those of our partners, without making them into a perceived disaster. It rarely is as catastrophic as we think. And as we learn to practice our imperfection skills, we can become more attuned to our relationship needs.

Optional Exercises

These exercises are designed to identify some common problem areas that may cause difficulties in your relationship. Be honest with yourself as you address your own take on these areas, and be kind to yourself along the way.

Things to Ponder

- How attached am I to doing things my way?
- Am I resistant to my partner doing things his (or her) way?
- Do I become easily annoyed because of the way my partner does things?
- Am I respectful towards my partner?
- Am I able to compromise in daily life situations?
- Have I considered the effects of mutual respect on my relationship?
- Do I have perfectionistic tendencies that need my attention?

Things I Can Do

- Make some notes about how I can develop mutual respect in my relationship.
- Talk to my partner about mutual respect and how it relates to harmony in the relationship.
- Take an inventory of things I need to be more aware of, and start working on them.
- Learn how to breathe when my partner is doing something annoys me.
- Read *The Gifts of Imperfection* by Brene Brown.
- Seek other books suitable to my relationship needs.
- Seek couple's therapy if needed.

CHAPTER 21

THE LANGUAGES OF LOVE

Love speaks in many ways!

Believe it or not, there are many ways in which people express their love to their nearest and dearest. However, it is not always recognised by the one on the receiving end, which can cause a whole lot of misunderstandings. The one expressing the love can be deeply hurt by the lack of gratitude or appreciation for what was intended by his or her gesture. The partner may not even realise that the gesture was an expression of love as it sailed right over his or her head. This is an interesting concept and one that many people would never think about. However, it is well worth getting an understanding of how we each have our own ways in which we express our love for each other. This understanding helps us to know what we do to express our love and what others do for us that make us feel loved. It also provides insight into recognising what makes our partners feel loved.

Some may have heard of Gary Chapman's popular book, *The Five Love Languages*. This book explains the different ways people demonstrate their love, and according to Chapman, they fall into five categories. The information in this book is priceless, and I recommend it as a useful resource to help you on your relationship journey. I'm highlighting this book as I believe it's a helpful resource in both choosing a partner and in the ongoing maintenance of the relationship. Over the years, I've heard many stories of how this book has improved people's relationships as it helps them understand their own and each partners' perspectives and intentions. I will endeavour to provide a brief outline of my interpretation of these love languages with some examples to enhance your understanding.

The five love languages encompass the many ways in which we express our love towards others and the different love expressions we receive from others that make us feel loved. Apparently, we all have our own primary love languages; sometimes more than one. The premise behind this theory is that we tend to use our own love languages to express our love to our partners. This means that if we have different love languages, we could be way off track in our love communications. Without knowing our partners' love language, we can misunderstand what they need, so they don't receive our intended love messages. Chapman places the five love languages under the headings: "Words of Affirmation," "Quality Time," "Acts of Service," "Receiving Gifts," and, "Physical Affection." These five descriptions contain all the possible love messages we can give to each other. I believe the first one is possibly the most important as it can very quickly either make or break a relationship.

Words of affirmation refers to the things we say to each other, how we say them, and the tone in which we speak. You are likely to be aware that our words can have huge consequences on the quality of our relationships. Our words give messages that can be kind and loving, or they can be harsh and unkind. Either way, they will have an impact, positive or negative. We can also give out messages that go way beyond the actual words that have been said based on the way we say them. Our tone and our words together give much stronger messages than words alone. They can amplify what we want to say. If we have a strong emotional charge behind what we are saying, the message can come through somewhat stronger than intended.

Words can be either intentional or unintentional. They may sometimes leave different messages rather than what they were meant to be portray. This can lead to people making wrong assumptions, which may lead to emotional pain and disharmony in the relationship. In doing so, communication becomes distorted, creating ongoing tension in the relationship. This sort of thing can happen so easily between couples. For example, your partner may be feeling a little vulnerable, and you may unintentionally say something insensitive. Your partner reacts negatively and triggers anger or annoyance in you. Then you raise your voice at your partner for misunderstanding you. This interaction may lead to ongoing conflict by fighting or stonewalling (ignoring your partner for an extended time). Or it could be calmed with an exchange of gentle and positive words that provide mutual support and understanding. Words have such power. They can determine the outcome of difficult situations, whether good or bad.

Harsh words can cause deep emotional pain, sometimes when the negative message was really not intended. The partner on the receiving end can react very negatively, confused by the mixed messages received because the one who is supposed to love him or her speaks harshly. They are likely to be thinking; *You don't love me because I'm obviously very annoying to you*, or, *I don't understand how you can speak to me like that,* and, *If you really loved me, you would speak nicely to me and not act like you hate me.* If we want to have a harmonious relationship, we need to stay mindful that the words we say and how we say them carry powerful messages that will have an impact.

I want to share another interesting point regarding the words we use towards each other. Pioneer marriage and relationship researchers, Drs. John and Julie Gottman found that it takes approximately five positive statements to counter one negative statement towards our partners. In other words, if we say something unkind to our partners, the damage will not be repaired until we've made five genuine positive comments. Some of the reactions I've heard from couples after sharing this fact have been most interesting. They include gestures such as raised eyebrows, darting looks at partners, sheepish guilty looks on faces, and comments such as, "Wow, you've got to be kidding me!" So seriously, take note if you want your relationship to run smoothly. If you take things out on your partner verbally, you may need to do some serious work before you restore the harmony in your relationship. An apology with a decent serve of humility, if needed, wouldn't go astray either!

The next love language is quality time, which is all about wanting to spend time with our partners, especially when we enjoy extra connectedness. This can also send positive or negative messages. It can be difficult when spending time together is important to one partner but doesn't mean much to the other. For example, if one partner likes to play golf and does so at every given opportunity when they don't have to work or do chores, and the other loves to have them around, even if they're just doing something around the house, the one who wants quality time is likely to feel rejected. In such cases, there can be a miscommunication in the love languages. The desire to play golf may send a message to the partner that golf is more important than she is, though it's more likely that he had energy to burn, loves his golf, and finds it a very good way to get some exercise. He most likely loves his partner very deeply and may assume she would understand his need to play golf. When love languages are known and shared, there is mutual understanding of what's really happening, leading to acceptance of the difference.

Acts of service is the next love language and refers to when our love is expressed by what we do for our partners. You will also feel loved when your partner does things to meet your desires and needs. A great example of this is when your partner brings you a coffee or tea first thing in the morning, and you wake up with that positive message of, "I feel loved!" I'm happy to say that I experience this every day as my husband has always brought a coffee for me first thing every morning. Acts of service covers many areas of the relationship. It includes doing housework, running errands, grocery shopping, doing repairs, and all those things that have to be done anyway. But the intention behind the action is to be doing your part for the household that is intended for the both of you. Of course, we all have different values about the way we live, and we will do things the way we like. But we have the intention of doing those things for the common good, expressing our love in this way.

The fourth love language is giving and receiving gifts. This also differs for everyone. Buying flowers for one's partner or receiving them may be the most loving gesture in the world for some, but for others, it could be a bit of a non-event. Have you ever met anyone who doesn't seem to appreciate receiving a gift? Earlier in my working life, I had a colleague who was having a special birthday, and a few of us decided to contribute toward buying her a gift. I was quite surprised when she seemed embarrassed; almost annoyed at the gesture. I think a more accurate word would be "awkward" rather than annoyed, but that's how it came across. I don't recall if she said, "Thank you," but I do remember her awkwardly pushing it aside and turning her attention to something else. I came to learn that she was not at all interested in material things. And when I learned about love languages, I realised that gifts scored pretty low on the scale for her. Alternatively, there are those who love to receive gifts, showing appreciation when perceived as loving gestures.

The fifth love language is about physical touch and affection. This applies to all kinds of physical contact, including a touch on the cheek, a stroke of the hair, or contact and enjoyment in the sexual relationship. Most men score high on this one as their sexual appetites are generally higher than women's—though not always—and they seem to enjoy more physical contact. I wonder if this becomes more pronounced when children come into the equation as the woman receives a lot of physical contact from her children during the day. It is common for the main caregiver to be exhausted by the time her partner comes home from work. In other cases, it seems that some people are just very affectionate by nature, and physical contact has always carried a lot of importance to them. Others can be indifferent, and in some cases, people can be tactile defensive and not like much physical contact at all.

Just being aware that we have differences in our worlds of love is enough to start a conversation. It's one of those times when we can be assured of a positive and loving interaction. It can be as simple as asking, "What sorts of things make you feel most loved?" I believe this can create a truly enjoyable conversation that results in finding out some interesting facts about ourselves and each other. Some couples enjoy reading the *Five Love Languages* book together and have benefited from taking turns reading a chapter aloud and then having a chat about it afterwards. Alternatively, you could both read it independently of each other. Either way, for those new to relationships, it's a good idea to have this information on your radar.

Understanding our love languages and the differences between our partners and ourselves has a huge impact on our relationships. It provides us with valuable information that helps us shift our expectations and let go of our preconceived ideas and incorrect interpretations that can cause misunderstanding. I trust this information will provide a bit of an understanding about how we express and perceive the love exchanges in our relationships.

Optional Exercises

The following suggestions will help you to learn more about how you give and receive love. They are designed to help you recognise what makes both you and your partner feel loved and how that works in your relationship. Exploring this can be light-hearted and fun!

Things to Ponder

- Do I know what makes me feel loved?
- Do I know what makes my partner feel loved?
- Have I given this area enough attention?
- Do I have one major thing or several things that make me feel loved?
- How can I find out what makes my partner feel loved?

Things I Can Do

- Get a copy of the *Five Love Languages* to read alone or with my partner.
- Do the test in the back of the book to identify my love language.
- Have a conversation with my partner to explore what makes him (or her) feel loved.
- Take notice of what I do for others to express my love for them.
- Ask other loved ones what makes them feel loved.
- Take specific notice of what sorts of things make me feel loved.
- Recognise when I am misinterpreting a love gesture from someone else.

CHAPTER 22

BEATING THE BLAME GAME

Blaming is just a bad habit that's well worth changing!

The intention of this chapter is about raising awareness of how the habit of blaming and shaming affects a relationship, and how often it's about things that are not so important. Of course, there are those times when a person is clearly at fault because he or she has done something wrong that harmed the relationship. In such cases, it's necessary for that person to take responsibility for his or her actions. These can include offences that are more on the serious side, such as having an affair, committing a crime, or engaging in acts of domestic violence. Such issues belong to another conversation altogether, so they are not addressed here. Instead, my focus is on that habitual tendency to blame someone every time something goes wrong. It's more of a habit that generally starts in childhood and follows into adulthood, causing havoc in relationships.

Let's face it, no one wants to be blamed for anything! When we're blamed for something that's gone wrong, it hits us where it hurts, making us feel bad or deficient in some way. When we hear someone say, "That was your fault," we immediately feel dreadful! We are blamed for causing harm to someone or something, which is never good. Then because we feel so awful, we may get into catastrophic thinking that makes us think we've done something really terrible, even if the situation was trivial. That thing can stay in our minds and bother us far longer than it should. We can become laden with guilt, and sometimes have to work really hard to climb out of those murky emotions to feel okay about ourselves. I will attempt to explain how this often unfolds for the person being blamed.

When a partner is blamed for something, what often follows is a dreadful sense of shame, causing the individual to then have both blame and shame to manage. These two strong emotions have damaging effects on that person's state of mind and psychological well-being. In reality, when strong emotions such as these are triggered, many others may emerge simultaneously, causing the person to feel overwhelmed.

Reactions generally depend on childhood experiences, which can make you vulnerable under certain conditions. For example, if early experiences included being humiliated and embarrassed, those emotions will emerge, creating two more emotions to manage. If you were bullied in the schoolyard, you may feel defeated, or if you were shamed for making mistakes by parents, teachers or others adults, you may feel a sense of failure, and so on. Through this process, many emotions can emerge just from being blamed.

When this happens, those who are overwhelmed with trying to manage this bundle of difficult emotions are likely to react in ways that are not helpful and, in fact, are often self-defeating. The possible reactions include getting into fight, freeze, or flight mode. When in fight mode, they may become angry and start fighting as a way of trying to defend themselves. If in freeze mode, they may feel trapped or stuck and not know how to deal with the situation. If in flight mode, they may be in denial or try to avoid addressing the situation altogether. These are very brief descriptions, but as you can see, they are all reactive. And none really add anything towards bringing peace to the situation. They also highlight how blaming can escalate ill-feelings in relationships, causing the conflict to extend unnecessarily.

Interestingly, there is often no need to assign blame to anyone because sometimes stuff just happens. Things gets broken or lost, mishaps occur, and items sometimes go missing for a time. However, it seems to be that when something goes wrong, there's often a need for an explanation, thinking that the situation demands an answer. So, to satisfy this perceived demand, there is an automatic tendency to assign blame. Unfortunately, because we don't want to take the heat ourselves, we usually direct the blame elsewhere. Why do we do this? The main reason is because we don't want to feel those awful negative feelings that come with blaming and shaming. Therefore, we deflect the blame elsewhere, even if it's towards someone we love. This pattern is commonly seen in couples, and generally, neither wants to give in, which reinforces the blame game. And the pattern continues over and over again in all kinds of situations.

However, if we take our attention away from blame for a moment and look at what the alternatives may be, we can begin to find some answers to this problem. The antidote to blaming and shaming others—or ourselves—is to look at the situation in a different way, one that leads us toward problem-solving. This requires taking a step back and looking more closely at the situation. And while we may find causes for the problem, we can also either solve it or accept it as a, "That's life," situation. Many things that go wrong in life are due to unintentional mishaps that can sometimes be explained by several contributors. Therefore, reaching for someone or something to blame is not the best way to go about problem-solving, but it is an automatic reaction that seems to happen spontaneously.

Of course, there are some cases that are clearly someone's mistake. Even so, there is no need to blame someone every time something goes wrong. The tendency to blame damages relationships when it's so unnecessary. A good example of this can be seen in families, especially with siblings who start playing the blame game when something goes wrong. They immediately start blaming each other. I'm sure everyone has heard such things as, "It was her fault!" or, "It was not! She did it. I saw her!" and, "You're a liar!" As funny as that can be at times with youngsters, it also happens between older kids, and young adults can continue this behaviour pattern into their adult relationships. We tend to take liberties with family and those we are closer to, becoming more open and critical of them. We can also be really good at making assumptions, and though we usually find out we've got things a bit wrong, we still tend to assume way too much without getting our facts straight.

If we take a philosophical perspective to see how this blame habit has evolved, consider the messages we received as children. For example, a mother is upset because she found a broken plate from her good dinner set in the cupboard. She may express her distress by yelling, "Who broke my plate?" Everyone recoils, and no one wants to fess up to breaking it. They may even say someone else did it for fear of being blamed.

A father may have misplaced his hammer and bellows, "Who's taken my hammer?" The same thing happens. Fear is evoked, and the kids just wish that hammer would show up because they don't want to get blamed for it. This kind of blaming in everyday life situations throughout childhood sets a pattern that resides within us and comes out automatically as a perception of how things must proceed when something is missing or goes wrong.

I believe this is why blaming and shaming are such ongoing problems in relationships. They are based on a pattern of behaviours that have been passed down and practiced throughout generations.

Remember, this is not about blaming our parents but is more an outcome of how things have carried on from one generation to another. We have somehow equated something going wrong with any old mistake or mishap needing to be someone's fault, when in fact, there could have been a reasonable explanation that does not include the need to blame. Because of this, many of us have grown up thinking that if something goes wrong, blame must be assigned to someone. This is nothing more than a bad habit, one that has become entrenched in our society. And it really needs to change!

When couples get into blaming each other on a regular basis, the love is often threatened, along with the relationship, sometimes leaving doubt about whether they want to be in the relationship any longer. The continued blaming in the transaction just ends up making matters worse, turning the situation into a much more serious problem. Sometimes this never gets resolved, and there are many relationship breakdowns in the world that can testify to this. The blame game shows up as a common problem in couple's therapy time after time. One partner will say, "He [or she] blames me for everything that goes wrong and never takes responsibility for anything!" The other partner may avoid commenting to prevent being blamed and shamed for behaving in that way. This may cause her [or him] to withdraw or fight back in some way, escalating the problem. Either way, the issue remains unsolved.

When someone makes a mistake or a mishap occurs and we get into blame mentality, we're not being fair on ourselves or our partners. And we bring disharmony into our relationships. If we can change our mindsets and remember that making mistakes is a normal part of being human that doesn't allow unnecessary blaming, things may be very different. As human beings, we all make mistakes, every one of us. It is part of the human condition. Whoever we are, we have made many mistakes in our lives before now and will continue to do so for as long as we live. This means that we need a better plan to deal with life when things go wrong. We need to put a stop to the blame game. If we don't want to be blamed ourselves, then it makes sense that we stop blaming others.

What if we were to look at things in terms of taking responsibility? If we are brave enough to take responsibility for our own actions, especially when things go wrong, we intercept the need for someone to blame us. We take it on the chin and can each apologise for our own part in creating the problem. Our mindset changes from blame to self-responsibility. That doesn't mean we take responsibility for others, but we simply own and fess up to our mistakes. In doing so, we can each provide a good role model with the potential to initiate change in this perception of blame and shame, leading to a healthier way of dealing with mishaps and providing a clear pathway to positive problem-solving strategies.

On the other hand, when we feel the need to blame someone else for something that's gone wrong, it may be helpful to stop and think; *Does someone really need to be blamed for this? Has something just gone wrong? Am I disappointed in some way?* Taking responsibility for our own thoughts and reactions is a part of the solution to this problem. When it comes to our relationships, this is far more meaningful as while we can walk away from many other situations, we don't want to do that in our relationships, especially over something trivial or unintentional. We want to create a happy environment in our relationships, and sometimes it's better to believe that just as we want our partner to believe in us, we need to support our partner. After all, they are probably doing the best they can, and we can't expect more.

Imagine how things would be if we all did away with blame and took responsibility for our own actions? What difference would that make in our lives? We would have no place for blame and, therefore, no shame that causes all those negative emotions to surface. Our energy and minds are freed to problem-solve and move on to the next thing—increasing productivity and improving relationships and connectedness along the way. This is so important in couple and family relationships and requires attention so we can change the way we look at ourselves, flaws and all, and be more accepting of who we are and less judgmental and more forgiving of others.

Optional Exercises

These suggestions are designed to overturn some of the negative actions and reactions you may have developed for when things go wrong. It is liberating and life-changing to take these concepts on board and see things a little differently, a task well worth taking.

Things to Ponder

- Do I have a habit of blaming others?
- If so, how did I develop that habit?
- Do I allow myself to be wrongly blamed for things?
- Did my family of origin engage in the blame game?
- How has blame adversely affected previous relationships?
- How do I behave when others make mistakes?

Things I Can Do

- Decide to start taking responsibility for my own mistakes and mishaps.
- Set my intention to avoid blaming others when things go wrong.
- Engage my problem-solving skills, and redirect my focus when things go wrong.
- Be quick to forgive others when they make mistakes.

- Be quick to forgive myself when I make mistakes.
- Be kind to myself and others when things go wrong in life.
- Take notice when things are trivial or non-intentional, and refrain from overreacting.
- Journal what I've learned from this chapter.

CHAPTER 23

ROLES AND RESPONSIBILITIES

Treat your partner in the same way you want to be treated.

From the moment we begin to share a home with another person, we will be faced with the task of working out how to keep the household running. In other words, who is going to be responsible for what tasks and chores to ensure everything gets done. Many relationships have become unstuck because one partner takes on too much, and the other one does way too little. This may seem a little mundane as a topic, and trust me, many people want to sweep this one under the carpet rather than actually cleaning it! This can turn into a significant problem if not addressed early on, and the imbalance can create a mammoth amount of tension in relationships. Also, it happens more often than I would like to recount that one partner is often totally oblivious to the damage being done.

It comes as quite a surprise when the partner taking on most of the responsibility brings it to the attention of the other and then has to deal with the pushback—because fighting about it may get you off the hook—which can be quite a challenge. The loafing partner will often interpret the situation as, "There she [or he] goes, nagging again. Get off my case! I'll do it when I feel like it! Don't tell me what to do. You're so controlling. Will you get off my back?" Yes, I have heard it all and could go on with this bottomless list of reactive retorts that come from partners who really don't want to pull their weight. If this is hitting a nerve with you, please understand that if ignored, this will not help your relationship and may not end well for you. By taking the blinkers off and being attentive to those things we need to address, we can reduce the tension in our relationships and have happier lives. Remember, "Happy spouse, happy house!"

Now I'm sure by now there is some cringing going on. But whatever you do, don't stop reading, as much as you may want to ignore this whole topic. Based on some of the situations that occur with couples, allowing yourself to be enlightened about this may just save your relationship. You may also be interested to know that generally, if we don't get this one right, it will follow us into the next relationship and the next. It will keep following us until we take notice or end up either very unhappy, alone, or both. Don't become a statistic in the cases of those broken relationships, where the bereaved partner later says, "I didn't see that coming. I was a good partner. Surely it wasn't that bad. What did I do wrong?" To answer that last question, perhaps that person didn't listen to their partner who left, but rather insisted on having things his or her way. When partners start slacking off on their share of the workload, their partners can become tired of hearing their own voices. And they may just give up and move on.

After completing my undergraduate studies in psychology, I was able to focus more closely on family and relationship issues. I was astounded to discover research findings that showed approximately 70 percent of men did not see the end of their relationships coming. The majority were so complacent about the roles they were required to play in their relationships that they were shocked when they received their marching orders. Alternatively, they may have come home to an empty house, and instead of finding dinner on the table, they found a note instead. Although these statistics were from over twenty years ago, I don't think this has changed much as I have consistently heard many similar comments since that time. Women can also find themselves in the same situation, though the statistics were much higher for men in the earlier research.

Unfortunately, the inequality of responsibilities in relationships occurs way too often. But by educating ourselves, we can prevent it from happening. Also, if it's already heading that way, we have the opportunity to make some much-needed positive changes. We don't like being taken for granted. Nor do our partners.

A great way to deal with this problem is to practice empathy in our relationships by putting ourselves in our partners' shoes at times and thinking about how things may be for them. For instance, we may see our clothes folded up and either in our drawers or on our bed, ready to be put away. It may be worthwhile to take a moment to think about how they got from being on the floor, crumpled and soiled, to being washed, dried, and folded neatly or put away. Alternatively, we may see our mates come home from work looking exhausted. It would be obvious that a lot of energy has already been spent for the day, and there may not be too much left. What would your mate need? Perhaps just some space, a walk or run outside, a need to debrief from the day, or sitting quietly with a glass of wine or a cup of tea. It's not always that easy when children are involved, but this can be problem-solved and alternatives made to suit each situation.

I've found that young couples, especially if they have children, are sometimes more likely to consider their own individual workload and related needs than to consider those of their mate. This makes total sense as it can be very difficult when there's a lot going on with the family and exhaustion starts to rule, leaving very little energy left to access our logical thinking brain to be able to problem-solve the situation. However, this is why addressing the issue of who is going to do what to keep things moving in the right direction is so important. It also makes sense to sort this issue out before children are involved, as getting this right in the beginning will help to make things work better in the future, when the family expands. Trust me, things will get more complicated!

Now then, let's get on to the nuts and bolts about roles and responsibilities. I hope we all know that there is a huge amount of work to be done to keep a household running smoothly. When we start working out responsibilities for each partner, it's important to consider all the tasks that need attention. There are the obvious housework tasks, which involve many chores. I won't mention them all here as they are numerous, but I should hope you would be aware to some extent that there are many chores to be done both inside and outside the house to keep things running smoothly. There are also bills to be paid and finances to manage, whether or not you have joint finances. Some households have pets that need to be taken care of, including walking them, feeding them, and taking them to the vet when needed. There is shopping to do and then hauling it home and putting it all away. I'm sure you get the gist. There is a lot to be done in one household, even with just two people.

The next issue I want to raise is that of personal preferences regarding cleanliness and tidiness in the house. You would be surprised at how many couples come unstuck with this one. It generally gets out of control when one partner likes things to be clean and tidy, and the other prefers to swim around in an array of messiness, where things are not put away but left out, cupboard doors are left open, shoes and clothes are left lying around on the floor, dirty washing is not in the hamper, and so on. This chaotic image is portrayed as being quite funny in some of the comedies we see in TV shows and movies, sometimes as being fully acceptable and other times as being totally annoying. However, as hilarious as it can be on the screen, it is not so funny in real life and can lead to an unhappy relationship consumed by ongoing disappointment, discontentment, and incredible frustration.

What generally happens in such situations is that while the differences may seem minuscule at the beginning of the relationships, frustration builds up over time until one of the partners becomes so fed up that he or she either leaves or threatens to leave. Either the tidy person gets sick of picking up after the one who likes to live in a mess, or the untidy one labels the partner as a "neat freak" and is opposed to any expectations and need to live in a more organised and cleaner environment. It's clear to see why we need to take notice of this issue, but some relationships will just not work out if the differences are too great and there is an unwillingness to listen to each other and compromise with what may be acceptable to both.

As a side note, it is worth mentioning here that when young couples start families with new babies coming into the house, there is a period right through to when the children are going to kindergarten or school that messes will need to be tolerated, no matter how neat you like to have things. During this time, parents can put a lot of pressure on themselves and sometimes their partners regarding the untidiness. We need to be kind to ourselves and each other and learn how to go with the flow. Our preferences will emerge later, and if they are compatible in the first place, the preferred way of living is likely to return. We have to make reasonable allowances at times, for example, when the population in the household expands. This includes when guests are staying.

When we enter a new relationship, it's worthwhile to look at this whole area and have a discussion about how things may look if the relationship moves into a longer-term situation. If there is no willingness to sort it out early, there could be some contention, with each partner standing their ground because they like to live a certain way and are not willing to compromise. When following the guidance found in some of the earlier chapters regarding discernment and compatibility, this is an issue that may have already been addressed. However, if you are already in a relationship and this is an issue for you, it's worthwhile to address it and understand that some compromising is needed to create some peace in this area. It really doesn't have to be a deal breaker and may bring some pleasing results.

A team approach works best when assigning roles and responsibilities, both before moving in together and then when the relationship has become more committed. It's well worth checking in at different times throughout the relationship until this issue becomes properly established, and things are running more smoothly. From my experiences, this area doesn't get enough attention when navigating a new relationship. I've been quite surprised at just how much of a problem it presents for couples, especially down the track. If this is not an issue for you, then great. You have compatibility in this area. But if you can see this is a problem area in your relationship, perhaps a discussion may be needed to work at getting on the same page with roles and responsibilities.

A good way of sorting this out is to make a list of all the tasks that need to be done to keep the household running smoothly. Include work commitments and extended family or other external commitments that may have demands on your time. Do this together so that it's a joint venture, and neither one is accused of dominating the situation. Then work out together a fair and reasonable distribution of tasks so that both partners know exactly what is expected of themselves and each other. Deal with any unrealistic approaches to this through each partner taking on individual responsibility. If it all has to be done, then why should you or your partner be doing most of the work? If you are stuck in an entrenched pattern due to the way you were raised, such as your mother doing everything for you, or having poor role models, you will do well to make some significant changes. Taking the initiative to make positive changes is incredibly empowering, especially when you own it and be responsible for your share of the work.

Optional Exercises

Sharing of responsibilities is important to address and will help get your relationship off on the right track. If you're already in a relationship, you may see some areas that need attention to keep things fair. The following will guide you through some considerations.

Things to Ponder

- Do I do too much or too little in my relationship?
- Was I raised having too much done for me?
- How did the way I was raised influence my approach to household duties?
- Do I think I have to do everything for others?
- Did my parents have problems with this and model unfairness?
- What things do I avoid and need to start facing?
- Am I hiding from this and ignoring the potential consequences?
- What changes may I need to make?

Things I Can Do

- Review my situation and plan changes I need to make.
- Share this information with my partner and consider any necessary changes.
- Map out all household duties and divide fairly.

- Take note of my actions and inactions and their consequences.
- Schedule time to do my chores and put them in my diary.
- Take responsibility for my roles so I don't need reminding.
- Keep things fair and don't be over-responsible, unless in special circumstances.

CHAPTER 24

COMMUNICATION SKILLS

Speak with integrity and listen wholeheartedly.

Poor communication is one of the major causes of problems in relationships and one of the main reasons many relationships do not survive. In other words, the relationship falls into a hole because the partners are unable to connect with each other in a way that helps them to really understand each other. I've heard many comments that go something like, "We just don't talk at all," or, "We just don't get each other," or, "We are just not on the same page!" These comments are all valid signs of poor communication. Such signs can appear in many relationships, even ones that seem to be surviving. The problem is that many people don't understand how communication really works in their relationships to help make and keep that healthy connection.

One common short-sighted theme regarding communication relates to the notion that it's all about talking to each other and the way in which we speak. This is certainly part of the communication process, but it's not all there is to it. It's in our best interests to know that there's much more we need to learn about the topic. The listening part gets swept over way too often, and the role that communication plays in the problem-solving process also gets lost in transition. Sometimes it's just way too important in the moment to get our points across. However, when we're in this state, we don't leave room to think about what may be happening for the other person. We're too consumed with our own thoughts to give that any space. Most problems can be either sorted or successfully reduced with effective communication. To achieve this, we need to make an effort to understand the processes of human interactions.

Basic communication is a two-way process that involves both talking and listening. As we now know, the talking part usually gets lots of attention, especially when it's coming from the one who is more outgoing and expressive or more emotionally charged. However, if the partner is more on the quiet side, he or she will usually remain silent, speaking only when prompted to answer. The less outgoing partner is likely to be taking everything in and may be too shy or afraid to speak. Some people like to take a sit back position, and in doing so, contribute to difficulties in their communication issues.

The problem with this scenario is that it's predominantly one-sided. There is no equality in the conversations, with only one partner having a say. It is necessary for both partners to have equal input in the talking process, which means both are given adequate time to have their say. It's equally important for both partners to learn and develop good listening skills. This means listening intently without thinking about what your response will be until you have thoughtfully processed what your partner has been saying to you. This is where many couples become unstuck in the communication process, as the dominant talker of the couple can have a habit of cutting the partner off before getting all the information.

In couple therapy situations, we like to teach people how to learn the skill of "active listening," which requires listening intently to what the partner is saying and then checking in with the partner afterwards about what they heard to make sure the meaning was clear. It's important that the right message is received so there is no misinterpretation. The thing that usually happens in this process is that people start jumping in and cutting off their partners in the middle of their talking time, and sometimes mid-sentence. At such times, we may use a "talking stick," which is an object, usually a decorated stick, that the person who is talking holds. The rule is that the person can only talk whilst holding the stick, while the other listens carefully without interrupting. Before responding, the one listening is prompted to provide feedback to his or her partner about what was heard before contributing to the conversation.

The talking stick is used in many situations, including group therapy, family meetings, and focus groups. It's an effective way of getting people to stop talking over each other. When considering how we often hear couples speaking to each other, you can imagine how well this works as an exercise. Some couples have adopted the strategy for use at home to help them stay on track, especially while they're trying to find their balance.

Another common complaint is, "He just won't talk." This mostly refers to the male partner but not always. After all, most of us women do like to talk! When the partner is more on the quiet side, he or she may need a bit of extra encouragement to speak, and the talking stick may help that partner find his or her voice. The listening part is also likely to require some practice, especially for those who are not used to their partners speaking up. It's also necessary for those on the shy side to have positive experiences when they eventually master speaking up. The partner is encouraged to hear what's going on for them and be able to draw more realistic conclusions for the subject at hand. When someone has a partner who doesn't speak up, he or she will tend to make assumptions and may misinterpret the situation.

When we are listening effectively, we are engaged and taking an interest in what the other person is saying. Keeping this in mind is helpful when learning to develop our communication skills. We can all get caught up with what's happening in our lives and have times when we don't listen properly. However, when we do, there are opportunities for both partners to exercise empathy as they gain an understanding of what is happening for the other, thus developing mutual respect. Making these changes can produce some amazing results for couples when their communication has been off track.

Communication also encompasses different ways of connecting with each other, including those non-verbal cues such as the way we look at each other and the way our body language forms its own expression of communicating. Such expressions can convey so much to our partners. It's true that a picture tells a thousand words, and those non-verbal communication cues can convey meaningful messages. We have the ability to either devalue our partners or boost their confidence with just a look or a gesture. The devaluing gestures include rolling our eyes, turning our attention away from them when they're trying to tell us something, ignoring them, giving disapproving looks, and being cold toward them. This is especially awful when it occurs in social situations and results in shaming the person we're supposed to love. If we want to let our partners know we love them and to boost their confidence in the relationship, we will act accordingly by showing warm affection, looking respectfully towards them, and responding to their words or actions.

We communicate certain things through what we say, how we say it, and how we respond to our partners. The tone in which we say things and the emotion behind that tone will have much to do with how the message is received. If you're feeling a little shaky at this point as you realise you've got some work to do in this area, don't be alarmed. None of us have this part nailed. As we are imperfect as humans and continually learning life lessons, we will all get this communication thing wrong at times. I'm the first to admit that this is an ongoing challenge in relationships; learning how to behave, speak, and respond in a respectful manner with each other. Even things that are said in jest can be hurtful and unwarranted at times. It takes time to develop this skill, so we need to be patient with each other while working on making the necessary changes. It also works best if we refrain from correcting our partners and focus instead on our personal growth.

It takes patience and self-responsibility from both partners for their communication skills to develop in a relationship. It also requires a level of maturity and the ability to hold a conversation, in which each person may need to accept their own part and be willing to be humble enough to own it and work through whatever it presents. This is one reason therapy is so important for some, as it encourages self-responsibility and provides a safe place for couples to be more honest and open with each other than they might be otherwise. Many couples acknowledge this fact when they attend therapy sessions together to work on their relationship. This is also a good reminder of why it's important to create a safe place for each other in the relationship. Having that sense of safety between partners encourages us to speak our minds more openly.

Let's now look at some of the obstacles that may get in the way of maintaining good communication skills. Our original unhelpful habits will always have the potential to come back and cause us grief. I'm including myself in this because I am fully aware that I'm just as likely as anyone else to get caught up with some of those old habits. There will be times when I will be shocked because I've noticed myself breaking my own rules. We sometimes get too busy to pay attention to what's going on, and at other times, our pride gets in the way. Hmmm, these things can really cause problems. For example, when life gets busy, we may find ourselves short-circuiting a conversation simply because we're tired and can't be bothered. In discussions, we can also get into that trap of wanting to be right, right? We talked about this earlier, and when there's a threat of not being right—or even worse, our partners being right—it can seem unthinkable at the time!

I hope you're having a quiet chuckle about yourself right now, like I am. This is a good one to be taking responsibility for, and I'm sure you've heard of humble pie. Well, this applies here, and if we're honest, there will be times in all our lives when we need to eat a piece of humble pie, which can be quite challenging. There are times we need to accept that we have gotten something wrong and that we are not always right! Interestingly, admitting our shortcomings can have the opposite effect from what we expect and is more likely to empower us, providing us with a sense of deep satisfaction for taking responsibility.

I trust you're aware by now that when we communicate with each other, it's not only about getting our own points across. It's also about learning how to really understand what's going on for our partners. The way in which we speak to each other conveys a specific message that can mean more than the message itself. We all know that if we're annoyed with someone, our tone is probably going to give us away, so we have to work a bit harder to prevent it from spilling out into angry outbursts. So how do we deal with this? We need to address the issues that are making us feel that way by speaking up about what's going on for us. This is what's happening, this is what I think, and this is how I am feeling. It requires engaging in an exchange of talking and listening as stated previously. We can't talk and listen at the same time, so let's not even try to do both at once.

The listening part requires that we not only listen to the words but also to the intention and emotion behind those words. We need to pay attention to any negative emotions such as frustration, disappointment, pain and sadness and also positive emotions such as happiness and contentment. When you take notice of what's really going on for your partner, you can become aware of what is needed in the relationship at a deeper level. This will make a significant difference to the quality in the relationship and help you get on the same page with each other. You will be able to engage in a more meaningful way, using empathy to both understand what you and your partner are experiencing.

Effective communication is required to develop healthy relationships. Too often, couples will engage in assuming what each other is thinking and feeling. We can't expect positive outcomes by making assumptions about each other because when we do that, we're more likely to get things wrong. When we're not sure about something our partners have said, we need to ask more questions until we have a full understanding of what they're trying to tell us. Asking further questions will have a positive impact on the outcome as it gives us a chance to get the full picture. Sometimes questions will help in situations where one partner is having difficulties explaining himself or herself. This provides a much better quality of communication compared with jumping in before your partner has had a say.

This chapter provided a snapshot of some of the most basic necessary communication issues that may help to get your relationship off to a good start. If you've had relationships or are in a relationship, then it will hopefully give you some ideas about how you can improve your communication skills. There is so much more to learn about communication and some great books on the topic. You may even want to engage in couple therapy or attend a relationship course with your partner to develop your communication skills. However, for the purpose of this book, I have aimed to provide guidance for new couples to promote a successful start to their relationships and for others to reflect on their communication skills and get some ideas on how to improve their connection.

Optional Exercises

If you're not currently in a relationship, the following suggestions will help you to explore and reflect on your communication style. If you are in a relationship, you may want to try out some new ideas so that you and your partner can improve your communication skills.

Things to Ponder

- Do I dominate conversations with my partner?
- Do I say too little in conversations with my partner?
- How do I do in the listening department?
- Do I dominate conversations with others?
- Do I hold back from speaking up in conversations in general?
- Do I need to make some adjustments in my communication skills?
- What non-verbal communication signs do I use?
- What non-verbal communication signs do I notice in my partner?

Things I Can Do

- Take more notice of how I interact with others.
- Take notice of how I interact with my partner.

- Reflect on how communication has affected previous relationships.
- Take positive steps towards getting the right balance in my communications with others.
- Be more aware of my part in conversations with others.
- Have a discussion with my partner or a close friend about communication skills.
- Explore and consider enrolling in a communication course for couples.
- Engage in couple therapy with an experienced therapist if needed.

CHAPTER 25

COMMITMENT, LOYALTY, AND BOUNDARIES

Commitment, loyalty and healthy boundaries are relationship essentials.

This chapter is written for those who are in more established relationships and does not apply to younger couples who are new to the dating game. However, it can be educational for anyone regarding future relationships when commitment is warranted for the survival of the relationship. Also, learning about boundaries is always a good thing, as we need to learn and practice good boundaries in all kinds of situations. Boundaries keep us safe, whether they are physical or emotional. This information may also provide insights regarding what may be needed in the future. Please keep this in mind while reading this chapter if you are new to the world of romance and relationships. For others who are in established relationships or between them, you may gain insights that improve your relationships.

Situations may occur, despite the couple being in a relationship for a reasonably long time, where one partner seems to remain half-hearted and not fully committed. This can cause the other partner significant anguish about where he or she stands. That partner is left unaware of the other's intention, often being confused about whether to stay or leave the relationship. I'm sure many have heard of this scenario at some time. We may ask; *What's that all about?* It could be that they are not fully convinced the relationship is right for them, it could be a pattern of behaviour, or there may be another underlying reason, causing the reluctance to commit.

If they are not comfortable with the idea of the relationship being right for them, it may be time to either take a break and think it through, or get some professional help. If it's a pattern of behaviour, it could be an indication that the person has an "Avoidant" attachment style. This was addressed in an earlier chapter on Attachment. If it's for any other reason, this will need to be explored to identify the cause of the inability to commit.

When one partner is unwilling to commit, he or she may avoid any discussions about taking the relationship to another level, whether it be moving in together, getting married, making a joint purchase of a home, starting a family, getting a pet, or any other initiative that has the potential to commit them further to the relationship. The other partner will struggle to understand and spend a lot of energy trying to figure out what's wrong. They may assume there's something about themselves that is causing the problem, leaving them confused and feeling bewildered and unloved. This can create or contribute to low self-esteem and can have damaging psychological effects that that can impact future relationships.

Reasons for reluctance to commit can include: incompatibility; loss of spark; fear of being alone; or feeling the need to please family or friends. The couple may have spent considerable time together and the relationship has become more of a habit than a desire to stay in for the long haul. It could be fear that exists due to coming from divorced parents. Whatever the issue, it's worth addressing as it's far better to know sooner rather than later if it's not going to work. The couple can then have the opportunity to either resolve the problem or bring it to an end. It's far better to get out of a relationship that's not working than to keep it going. This is because while staying in the relationship, there is little chance of moving on to something else that's mutually beneficial, such as each finding relationships with more compatible partners.

Loyalty is another requirement for developing successful relationships. This is a two-way process and involves the couple forming a deeper level of commitment to each other in various ways. The most obvious way, of course, is staying loyal in intimacy. I don't know many couples who are okay with their partners having other sexual partners. In many cases, this is a deal-breaker that will end the relationship. Many people say the one thing they will not tolerate or forgive is their partner being unfaithful. Deep hurt and resentment results when partners have been disloyal and unfaithful by having an affair. This may also include situations where a partner has come close to leaving the relationship for another love interest. In such situations, while some recover, many don't, and the aggrieved partners are left with deep scars of sadness that don't shift easily and can remain for a long time.

Anyone who's been cheated on while in a relationship knows how devastating this can be; crushing to the soul. Apart from having been through this myself in a previous relationship, I've seen many people in therapy following affairs, some individually and others in couples. The evidence of heartache and suffering is always present. In some cases, there's also a considerable amount of anger and hostility. While forgiveness is often sought by the offending person, this doesn't come easily for the partner, and sometimes the relationship has to end because of the inability to rebuild trust. This topic is covered here because once this line is crossed, it is definitely not easy to recover from the injuries. After seeing many people at various stages of this painful process, including numerous offenders who were filled with remorse, I strongly recommend that couples take their commitment and loyalty to their relationships seriously.

If an affair has occurred, the offender needs to take responsibility for his or her actions. Many will place the blame elsewhere, including on their partners. There are some offenders who will do anything to avoid taking responsibility. I've also found that some will downplay the affair and bolster justification for their actions. They can be unwilling to try and understand the pain their actions caused their partners and to the security of their relationships. However, if they want to repair their relationships, they will need to take responsibility for their actions. If this is not dealt with honestly and openly, it will likely cause ongoing problems later. If you believe something is missing in the relationship, it is best to deal with that instead, and either sort things out or end the relationship. It's best to be honest and upfront, especially if you know you're unable to stay faithful.

Other ways in which loyalty matters in relationships relates to couples supporting each other and standing strong together. I'm astounded at how many stories I've heard of interference coming from parents or siblings. This sometimes influences the son or daughter to be swayed toward joining forces with the family member instead of managing the issues with their partner. And this does not refer to providing support when needed, but by deliberate interference due to someone else thinking they know what's better for you. In marriage or any committed relationship, this matter of loyalty is so important. Couples need to communicate and connect as a united team—without interference from others. It's up to each partner to ensure this happens. Couples deserve the right to be able to move on with their relationships, making their own decisions together. They can always ask for help or advice if they need it; this is a practice I always encourage in couples.

Commitment and loyalty are associated with healthy boundaries, which are needed to keep us safe and on task with the different relationship roles we develop throughout life. Boundaries are violated when couples allow others to interfere in their relationship. The bond between the couple is injured and this will cause problems until addressed. When we adhere to healthy boundaries in our relationships, we promote healthy connections. It may be necessary in some cases to lovingly remind mothers and fathers that though we love and need them in our lives, we no longer require their role as parents. The role of mother or father is very different to that of the parent—and although difficult—this sometimes needs explaining. Interestingly, many parents are as just as relieved to hear this as their adult children!

Some people have a lot of trouble with boundaries, mostly due to growing up with few or no boundaries in their family of origin. Consequently, they are left to learn about them later, usually after they've been adversely affected in some way. A good way of getting your head around this is to imagine a paddock or a house with fences around it, and then imagine being within that space together with your partner. Others are in their respective places outside your boundaries, yet still connected. This can make boundaries appear more real, enabling us to respect them and know they are there to promote safety—along with the nurturing and development of your relationship. It pays to start working on this issue reasonably early in the relationship. If there are problems with boundaries, they will escalate when children come into the equation.

For families where children are involved, boundaries can be disrupted through situations in which one child's been given too much reign in the family and is ruling the roost. My days of running parenting groups showed this continuously in situations where everyone in the family dances around the demands and expectations of one child. When this happens, the whole family is thrown into chaos as the boundaries have become blurred, and the household is continuously disrupted. A major problem with this situation is that it puts the child in a compromised position. No child is equipped to deal with the responsibility of being in charge of the family. This can cause the child an underlying sense of feeling unsafe that may present as anxiety, sometimes camouflaged as disruptive behaviour.

In most cases, parents are unaware of what's happening and continue to reinforce the pattern, remaining oblivious to the source of the problem. When recognised, the family dynamics can shift to put the parents back in charge of the family—creating the emotional safety the child requires. Boundaries are necessary to keep harmony in the home, and this requires a parental alliance that is stronger than the will of a child who may be struggling due to being out of his or her depth. Some great parenting books are available that provide good guidance for promoting child development. Parenting courses are also a great way to address parenting issues as they get parents on the same page, enabling them to take a step back and look at the situation. This provides an opportunity to develop the skills needed to make any necessary changes and also recognise what's going well.

This chapter provides general information for promoting and maintaining healthy relationships. However, there are exceptions to remaining loyal in a relationship; this is mainly when domestic violence is involved. It is not recommended to stay in a relationship where domestic violence exists in any form. Under such conditions, support may be needed from trusted family, friends, or professionals to help the affected person get out of the situation. Loyalty does not belong to someone who is abusive towards us in any way. Boundaries are not designed to trap anyone into an abusive relationship. In such cases, personal boundaries are needed to keep ourselves safe. This includes finding ways to remove ourselves from that relationship. We need to be in a safe relationship before we can establish healthy boundaries. And if you realise you're not safe, it may be time to strengthen those personal boundaries and seek help.

One final note and reminder: The purpose here is to provide some basic psycho-education about relationships and prepare you with the best chances of success. It should also provide understanding of some things that may cause problems down the track. If you have concerns about your relationship, you may need to seek professional help to address your personal needs regarding your individual situation. Relationships will always present with problems and challenges, most of which can be overcome with the help of some of the skills presented in this book—and looking further afield. The most important thing is to aim at getting things the best you can in the first place by making sound choices that keep you empowered while providing the opportunity to enjoy healthy relationships.

Optional Exercises

These suggestions will prompt your attention towards your level of commitment to relationships past and present. They will also help to identify issues you may have, help you to identify any loyalty issues, and prompt you to check your boundaries.

Things to Ponder

- Do I have a sound commitment to my relationship?
- Does my partner show commitment to the relationship?
- Do I have a good understanding of what commitment to a relationship means?
- Have I grasped the concept of loyalty and what that means?
- Do I need to take any action regarding loyalties?
- Do I have sound boundaries both personally and in my relationships?
- Do I need to take steps to improve boundaries in my life?

Things I Can Do

- Discuss any commitment issues with my partner.
- Consider my personal ability to commit to a relationship.
- Take steps to seek help if I am avoiding commitment to any relationships.
- Discuss with my partner any identified issues regarding loyalty.
- Instil healthier boundaries in my relationship if needed.
- Identify and address issues regarding interference from others.
- Continue working on boundaries and keeping them healthy.

CHAPTER 26

STAYING TRUE TO YOUR SOUL PURPOSE

Be true to yourself in your relationship, and maintain your soul purpose.

Through the many lessons presented in this book, we can learn all about relationships, receive guidance to follow along the way, and develop all the skills required to cultivate and keep a good relationship. None of it really matters, however, if you are unable to maintain your sense of self in your relationship. You owe it to yourself, to your soul purpose in life, and to all that you know of who you are to be your best authentic self. You can only do this if you are able to remain true to yourself in your relationship. If you can't be authentic in your relationship, you'll be setting yourself up for facing some difficult times ahead. This is why the question of whether or not you can be yourself in a relationship is so important. As emphasised throughout this book, there is a reason it really pays to do our individual work first and have that securely in place before we embark on getting into a relationship.

In the earlier chapters in this book, I focused consistently on the importance of being true to yourself. I provided further information about what this means when we get into relationships. I've also written about how people can lose themselves in their relationships, giving up who they are to conform to their partners' ways. A sure sign of this is when comments come from friends and family like, "I don't know what's happened to her," or, "He seems to have completely lost himself." I have even heard grieving friends and family members say, "We don't know her anymore. We've lost her!" Anyone who is in this type of situation through getting into a relationship will struggle to maintain a sense of self and consequently struggle to stay with their true soul purpose.

I believe we are all on a journey in this life. We each have our unique path to take which I refer to as our "soul purpose." Whether or not we are in a relationship, we owe it to ourselves to be invested in nurturing our individual selves. This is what will lead us to finding our unique soul purpose in life. If we do happen to be in a relationship either now or in the future, it pays to develop a shared understanding about this with our partners. Sometimes this just happens naturally and is evident by the support each partner gives the other. A certain amount of empathy is required from each partner to understand that while something may not on a personal level seem important, it may be to our partner. Therefore, a compromise may be required to support our partner while maintaining our own journey.

Something I realised a long time ago is that no one knows exactly what another person's soul purpose is, no matter how close they are to that person. It can take us a lifetime to work it out for ourselves. We come into this world alone, and we leave it on our own. Therefore, it's up to each of us to be true to who we are and not allow ourselves to compromise this for the sake of others. This is how we are able to maintain engagement with our soul purpose. It would be tragic to waste precious opportunities in our lives by allowing ourselves to become what we think others want us to be. If you allow yourself to become an extension of another, you will lose the unique essence of who you are in the relationship.

Being our authentic selves is important in all our relationships. It will help us to maintain a healthy sense of who we are, enhancing our lives while allowing us to maintain self-respect and to treat others respectfully in the process. This will determine the quality of all our relationships, but especially those we connect with romantically. We never really know when we start a relationship whether it will be short term or for the rest of our lives. This is all part of the mystery of getting to know someone as we venture further into the relationship. If we do this well and are authentic from the start, we are likely to realise earlier whether or not the relationship is worth continuing.

When we are young, we venture into the world of relationships, often with plans to have children and form families of our own. Most often things start out ticking along okay, but then things can go awry years down the track. Sometimes there's a bitter divorce, causing chaos, depleting finances through legal disputes, and the very worst of all, children being caught in the middle of custody battles. Too many children witness nasty interactions between their parents, both of whom they love deeply and want to make happy. This becomes part of the children's journey, and they will need to get through all their own pain before they are available to figure out their own soul purpose in life. This is not always so bad as hardships have allowed many of us to each develop our unique character and do good in the world. But then there are also casualties with those who don't survive so well.

It pays to choose wisely when you're looking for that special person in your life. You need someone who allows you to be yourself, who supports and encourages you in all the things that matter to you. In return, you can do the same for that person. Even if you don't plan to have children, the principles still apply. When we're young, we can be impulsive and impatient, and it's easy to get into relationships for all the wrong reasons. It could be about looks, status, financial security, pleasing others, keeping a friendship circle together, or some other relatively superficial reason.

If you are reading this and it is resonating with you, this book is written for you. My intention is to provide practical guidance in making better decisions about who you'll choose for a life partner. This has the potential to increase the chances of keeping your family together and give you a better life in the process, while enabling you to achieve your true potential in the life for which you are destined.

Life doesn't always turn out as we plan. However, just because things don't always run smoothly, they can still turn out okay and sometimes even turn out better than our original plans. In the arts, there's an understanding that mistakes will sometimes take an ordinary painting or a song to another level, showing a brilliance that wouldn't have been found otherwise. Life can also be like that sometimes—after all, don't forget those wonderful silver linings. Much good can come out of failed relationships. Therefore, if you've had a few relationship disappointments, don't despair. You have the opportunity to change your approach to relationships and put your energy into something positive. With a little knowledge, insight, and effort, you can become empowered to turn your life around. That is all within your power!

When we do the individual work on ourselves as explained in Part 1, we're better placed to know ourselves so much better than before and will be well equipped to express ourselves in authentic ways; this also benefits others who come into our lives. When we commit ourselves to grow and develop into healthier adults, and learn how to maintain the practice of looking after ourselves, we're more likely to be successful in all our relationships. As we learn how to be discerning in choosing our partners, as described in part 2, we can attract those we are more compatible with, that will enable us to stay true to ourselves while developing and maintaining fulfilling relationships.

This applies to everyone, but especially to those like me, who came out of a dysfunctional family of co-dependency with poor relationship role models. Our experiences taught us the habits that led us to attract the wrong people into our lives. Through my years of working as a therapist, I've become aware of hundreds of experiences similar to mine. Many of us grew up not knowing what a healthy relationship looks like. However, that doesn't mean we can't learn how to have one. Whatever we've learned, even when we were young, we can unlearn and find new ways of doing things. And remember, there is no such thing as a perfect relationship. No matter how good our relationship is, we will always have some challenging times that will throw us and require some sorting out.

Inevitably, there will be arguments and disagreements over all kinds of things. This is normal, especially when we're still getting to know each other. We just need to remember some of those basic relationship principles, to be fair and kind to each other, and to have a shared understanding of the need to get on the same page to resolve each challenge. Having a shared understanding that things will not always go smoothly will help couples develop more realistic expectations. If we view things from the perspective that there are consequences for all our decisions, we can keep ourselves humble by taking responsibility for the role we play in our relationships. There is so much more to learn about relationships, and these snippets of information are really just a starting point as early in our relationships, most of these things are not known.

Some have asked me why relationship education is not taught in high schools, to which, of course, I have no answer. I'm not sure anyone knows the answer to that one! However, I will certainly celebrate the day when I hear of this happening. In the meantime, this has been the main purpose of part 3. I have aimed to provide a brief starter course on relationships, including what works best, what causes problems, and how to prevent things from going wrong. It is designed to provide some answers when people are unsure of what questions to ask and provide guidance in the things that really matter. Of course, there's so much more information to be found on every topic mentioned in this book. I encourage people to read further afield where needed.

In conclusion, when you are connected to your soul purpose, you are getting in touch with the very core of your being. This is where you will find your light and true worth. Goodness knows we need more light in this world, so stay true to yourself, and let yourself shine, so you can be the unique person you are meant to be. This will enhance your life and the lives of all others whose lives you'll touch. Most of all, it will keep you empowered!

REFERENCES

Part 1

Aisbett, Bev (2010). *I love me: A guide to being your own best friend.* Sydney, Australia: Harper Collins Publishers.

Brown, Brene (2017). *Braving the wilderness: The quest for true belonging and the courage to stand alone.* London, UK: Penguin Random House.

Brown, Brene (2015). *Rising strong: If we are brave enough, often enough, we will fall. this is a book about getting back up.* London, UK: Penguin Random House.

Brown, Brene (2010). *The gifts of imperfection: Let go of who you think you're supposed to be and embrace who you are.* Minnesota, USA: Hazelden.

Brown, Nina (2001). *Children of the self-absorbed: A grownup's guide to getting over narcissistic parents.* Oakland, California, USA: New Harbinger.

Dispenza, Joe (2012). *Breaking the habit of being yourself: How to lose your mind and create a new one.* Carlsbad, California USA: Hay House.

Hay, Louise (1999). *You can heal your life.* Carlsbad, California, USA: Hay House.

Neff, Kristin (2021). *Fierce Self Compassion: How women can harness kindness to speak up, claim their power, and thrive.* New York, USA: Harper Wave.

Neff, Kristin (2011). *Self Compassion: Stop beating yourself up and leave insecurity behind.* London, UK: Yellow Kite.

Webb, Jonice, and Musello, Christine (2014). *Running on empty: Overcome your childhood emotional neglect.* New York, USA: Morgan James Publishing.

Young, Jeffrey E., and Klosko, Janet S. (1994). *Reinventing your life: The breakthrough program to end negative behaviour and feel great again.* New York, USA: Plume Books.

Part 2

Beattie, Melody (1990). *The language of letting go: Daily meditations for codependents.* Minnesota, USA: Hazelden.

Beattie, Melody (1986). *Codependent no more: How to stop controlling others and start caring for yourself.* Minnesota, USA: Hazelden.

Bowlby, John (1988). *A secure base: Clinical application of attachment theory.* London, UK: Routledge.

Dyer, Wayne W. (2004). *The power of intention: Learning to co-create your world your way.* Carlsbad, California, USA: Hay House.

Fisher, Bruce and Alberti, Robert (2016). *Rebuilding: When your relationship ends.* Oakland, California, USA: New Harbinger.

Golomb, Elan (1995). *Trapped in the mirror: Adult children of narcissists in their struggle for self.* New York, USA: Harper.

Levine, Amir, and Heller, Rachel S. F. (2019). *Attached: Are you anxious, avoidant or secure? How the science of adult attachment can help you find—and keep—love.* London, UK: Bluebird.

Mazzola, Krystal (2019). *The codependency recovery plan: A 5-step guide to understand, accept and break free from the codependency cycle.* California, USA: Althea Press.

Norwood, Robin (1985). *Women who love too much.* London, UK: Arrow Books.

Part 3

Brown, Brene (2012). *Daring Greatly: How the courage to be vulnerable transforms the way we live, love parent and lead.* London, UK: Penguin Random House.

Chapman, Gary (1992). *The five love languages: How to express heartfelt commitment to your mate.* Chicago, USA: Northfield Publishing.

Clear, James (2018). *Atomic Habits: An easy & proven way to build good habits & break bad ones.* London, UK: Penguin Random House.

Gottman, J., Gottman, J., Abrams, D. and Abrams, R. C. (2019). *Eight dates: Essential conversations for a lifetime of love.* New York, USA: Workman Publishing.

Gottman, J., Gottman, J. and De Claire J. (2006). *Ten lessons to transform your marriage.* New York, USA: Three Rivers Press.

Gottman, J., and Silver, N. (2015). *The seven principles for making marriage work: A practical guide from the country's foremost relationship expert.* New York, USA: Harmony Books.

Hendrix, Harville and Hunt, Helen LaKelly (2019). *Getting the love you want: A guide for couples.* New York, USA: St Martin'sGriffin.

Johnson, S. (2008). *Hold me tight: Seven conversations for a lifetime of love.* New York, USA: Little, Brown and Company.

EPILOGUE

Thank you for purchasing and reading this book. It was a book that had to be written! The intention is to provide sound guidance to you in the quest of your relationship journey. My hope is that you received from it what you need to enhance your relationship with yourself and others. I sincerely trust the insights you gained will guide you throughout your life to make a difference to you and those you bring into your life.

Please feel free to visit me at www.wendyjbritten.com for updates. You can also follow my blog, sign up for my newsletter and access the free meditations, which are available on the – *Resources* – page of my website.

Relationships are so important as it's through them that we get to express our love toward others and also learn about how we can love ourselves. Therefore, putting the energy into laying the groundwork for our relationship journey is well worth the effort.

I would like to leave you with the following quote:

A healthy relationship is when two people
can be authentic with each other.
They don't have to hide who they are,
They don't need to pretend to be what they're not.
Their mutual love and respect for each other
keeps their relationship steadfast!

—Wendy J. Britten

CPSIA information can be obtained
at www.ICGtesting.com
Printed in the USA
BVHW072322180523
664414BV00001B/48

9 781982 295981